# CONFIDENCE
# AND DOMINION

# CONFIDENCE AND DOMINION

## AN ECONOMIC COMMENTARY ON PSALMS

GARY NORTH

POINT FIVE PRESS
*Dallas, Georgia*

*Confidence and Dominion: An Economic Commentary on Psalms*

Copyright © 2012, 2021 by Gary North

*Published by*
Point Five Press
P.O. Box 2778
Dallas, Georgia 30132

Typesetting by Kyle Shepherd

*This book is dedicated to*

*Robert Thoburn*

*whose optimism has been constant*

# TABLE OF CONTENTS

*The irreversible Kingdom of God in history.*

# INTRODUCTION

The Book of Psalms is the premier book on optimism in the Bible. As such, it is the premier book of optimism in the ancient world. Nothing else comes close.

While many psalms are anguished cries regarding the psalmist's sinful condition, the book presents a picture of *the irreversible kingdom of God in history*. There is nothing in Psalms that even hints at the possibility that God's kingdom will not transform the whole world.

The basis of this optimism is God's covenant with Israel. This covenant has a structure. This structure rests on five principles: the absolute sovereignty of God; His delegation of authority to redeemed representatives of His kingdom; the Bible-revealed laws of God; the sanctions—positive and negative—that are inescapably bound to God's law; and the comprehensive inheritance in history of His people.[1]

This optimism has implications. God expects covenant-keepers to maintain confidence that *their lives will positively transform the world to the extent that they conform themselves to God's Bible-revealed laws. The future is not booby trapped by God to threaten covenant-keepers. It is booby trapped by God to threaten covenant-breakers. **History is not a level playing field. The contest between the kingdom of God and the kingdom of Satan is rigged against Satan.*** From Genesis 3:5 to Revelation 22, this is the message of the Bible. Until you accept this, you will never understand the Bible.

Entrepreneurship is an economic term that applies to people's (1) forecasting of the economic future and (2) designing plans to meet that future with a minimal expenditure of scarce resources. In

---

1. Ray R. Sutton, *That You May Prosper: Dominion By Covenant*, 2nd ed. (Tyler, Texas: Institute for Christian Economics, 1992), chaps. 1–5. Gary North, *Unconditional Surrender: God's Program for Victory*, 5th ed. (Powder Springs, Georgia: American Vision, 2010), chaps. 1–5.

1

four words, it is this: *buy low, sell high*. But entrepreneurship applies to all areas of life, not just the money economy. Everyone must deal with the future. The covenant-keeper is to buy low in the broadest sense, and also sell high in this sense. He is supposed to use the resources that God has granted to him as tools of kingdom-extension. The greater his confidence in the success of his efforts, the more likely he is to commit to a program of investing. He must invest time, money, and emotional commitment to the Great Commission.

> And Jesus came and spake unto them, saying, All power is given unto me in heaven and in earth. Go ye therefore, and teach all nations, baptizing them in the name of the Father, and of the Son, and of the Holy Ghost: Teaching them to observe all things whatsoever I have commanded you: and, lo, I am with you alway, even unto the end of the world. Amen (Matt. 28:18–20).[2]

This commission involves far more than bringing the message of personal salvation through Christ's redemption (repurchase). It involves the redemption of the world.[3] It involves *the replacement of sin with righteousness in every area where sin now reigns*. Sin is not given an eschatological King's X until the final judgment. Satan is not given a free ride. The Christian gospel, when it preaches the Bible, is a comprehensive gospel.[4]

A person who is convinced that this task is impossible, according to the Bible, is not going to make the same degree of commitment as a person who sees his efforts as part of a program ordained by God for success. *This is why confidence is crucial for success*. This is not self-confidence. It is confidence in a foreordained plan of God. Psalms presents the broad scope of this comprehensive program of cultural victory. No other book in the Bible rivals it in this regard.

Psalms is a didactic literary work, not primarily an historical work. It is intended to persuade. It is not an historical work in which there are literary activities mentioned, unlike the Old Testament's historical books or the Book of Acts. It is also not a prophetic work, set in specific times with an accompanying historical narrative. I therefore use the present tense when describing what the psalmists wrote. They wrote in the past, but their message was directed at covenant-keepers

---

2. Gary North, *Priorities and Dominion: An Economic Commentary on Matthew*, 2nd ed. (Dallas, Georgia: Point Five Press, [2000] 2012), ch. 48.

3. Kenneth L. Gentry, *The Greatness of the Great Commission: The Christian Enterprise in a Fallen World* (Tyler, Texas: Institute for Christian Economics, 1990).

4. Gary North, *Is the World Running Down? Crisis on the Christian Worldview* (Tyler, Texas: Institute for Christian Economics, 1988), Appendix C.

throughout history. A didactic literary work is written for a particular era, but it is also expected to convey its message down through the ages. The psalmists spoke to their contemporaries, yet they also speak to us as contemporaries. Their words should be treated as contemporary.

Covenant-Keeper is supposed to use the resources that God has granted to him as tools of Kingdom-extension.

Need confidence in victory - progress

Must invest time, money & emotional commitment to the Great Commission.

— more than bring message of personal salvation through Christ's redemption.
+
⹀ redemption of the world.

— It involves the replacement of sin with righteousness in every area where sin now reigns

— Know & believe in a fore ordained plan of God.

Psalms presents the broad scope of this comprehensive program of cultural victory.

No other book in the Bible rivals it in this regard.

Psalms - meant to persuade.

*Righteous person will prosper in whatever he does.*

# 1

# INDIVIDUAL ETHICAL CAUSE AND EFFECT

*Blessed is the man that walketh not in the counsel of the ungodly, nor standeth in the way of sinners, nor sitteth in the seat of the scornful. But his delight is in the law of the Lord; and in his law doth he meditate day and night. And he shall be like a tree planted by the rivers of water, that bringeth forth his fruit in his season; his leaf also shall not wither; and whatsoever he doeth shall prosper. The ungodly are not so: but are like the chaff which the wind driveth away.*

PSALM 1:1–4

## A. Theonomy and Causation

The theocentric issue here is God's law. The Book of Psalms begins with an affirmation: the righteous individual who avoids contact with evil individuals is blessed. The psalm says that an individual must not sit in the seat of the scornful or scoffers. These people are contemptuous. Contemptuous of what? God's law. In contrast, the righteous individual delights in the law of God. He meditates on the law day and night. He studies the law of God and thinks about how it should be applied in specific circumstances. He does not simply study the law as an academic exercise. He studies God's law in order to become an expert in rendering judgment.

This psalm describes such an individual as being like a tree planted by the rivers of water. A tree planted by water produces fruit according to the proper season. It does not wither prematurely. It has access to water. The tree does not dry up. The analogy of a tree planted by the water applies to *a life that is productive because it does not lack an important resource*. Therefore, the psalmist says, the righteous individual will prosper in whatever he does.

*Tree planted by the water — A life that is productive because it does not lack an important resource.*

5

*[handwritten: ethics ←→ prosperity]*

*[handwritten: Productivity]*

This affirmation is designed to increase men's faith in the predictability of their environment. There is a cause-and-effect relationship between ethics and productivity. *There is a positive sanction for righteousness: prosperity.* An individual who is ethically righteous has an advantage over an evildoer. The righteous individual finds that he is blessed by God with greater wealth. *This gives him a competitive advantage.*

This is in contrast to the ungodly individual. Such an individual is like the chaff which the wind blows away. The symbolism here is that of winnowing or separating wheat from chaff. In a windy environment, a harvester tosses wheat and chaff into the air. The chaff weighs less than the wheat, so the wind blows the chaff away. This leaves wheat, which is a valuable resource. Chaff is not.

The psalmist says that the ungodly individual is like the chaff. He will not prosper. So, to the extent that individuals conform themselves to the law of God, they become the owners of greater resources than those people who disobey God's law. The psalmist specifically says that "the Lord knoweth the way of the righteous: but the way of the ungodly shall perish" (v. 6).

This is a short psalm. The psalmist is making a major covenantal point. He applies to the individual the same cause-and-effect system of ethics that Moses said applies to a nation. In Deuteronomy 28, Moses set forth a list of the sanctions that apply to nations. Righteous nations prosper; unrighteous nations do not. Leviticus 26 affirms the same cause-and-effect relationship. The Mosaic law rested upon a particular view of causation. It affirmed faith that righteousness is blessed, and unrighteousness is cursed. *The world around us is predictable in terms of the ethics and historical sanctions of the Mosaic law.*

The psalmist here affirms that biblical law is the correct standard of ethics. He also affirms that this ethical standard produces predictable effects for individual behavior. If an individual seeks prosperity, he should conform himself to the comprehensive, Bible-revealed law of God. If he wishes to avoid the negative sanction of poverty, he should avoid violating the laws of God. Covenant-keepers who conform themselves to biblical law have a competitive advantage over covenant-breakers who violate it. Leviticus 26 and Deuteronomy 28 affirm this with respect to corporate groups. This psalm affirms it with respect to individuals.

Covenant - Keepers produces blessings in history.

## B. Individual Self-Interest

Psalm 1 teaches that covenant-keeping produces blessings in history. In contrast, covenant-breaking produces losses in history. An individual who is self-interested should therefore conform himself to the Bible-revealed laws of God. *Biblical law*

This psalm does not affirm righteousness solely as an end in itself. It affirms righteousness in terms of *individual self-interest*. It begins with the phrase, "blessed is." It assumes that individuals prefer blessings to curses. They prefer positive sanctions to negative sanctions. To the extent that an individual prefers blessings over curses, he should study the Bible-revealed laws of God and then seek to apply them consistently to the environment around him. This is not to say that the comprehensive law of God should not be appreciated for its inherent qualities. An individual is to delight in the law of the Lord, the psalmist says. There is a delightful element about the consistency of God's law. But such delight is not limited to aesthetic enjoyment or intellectual satisfaction. It is preliminary to action. An individual is not simply to be a hearer of the law; he is to be a doer of the law (James 1:22).[1] When he is a doer of the law, he positions himself to be a recipient of positive sanctions.

The existence of positive sanctions points to the fact that individuals want to be practical. They do not wish to act against their own self-interest. God has created an environment for mankind that rewards covenant-keeping. This provides an added incentive for an individual to study the laws of God. It is not sufficient that the laws of God are consistent with each other, and that they present a comprehensive system of government, beginning with self-government. Obedience to these laws must also produce positive sanctions. These sanctions reinforce man's confidence in the legitimacy of the laws of God. As Moses put it, "But thou shalt remember the LORD thy God: for it is he that giveth thee power to get wealth, that he may establish his covenant which he sware unto thy fathers, as it is this day" (Deut. 8:18).[2]

The unrighteous individual does not believe this. To the extent that he believes in an ethical cause-and-effect universe, he believes that unethical behavior produces greater blessings than righteous be-

---

1. Gary North, *Ethics and Dominion: An Economic Commentary on the Epistles* (Dallas, Georgia: Point Five Press, 2012).

2. Gary North, *Inheritance and Dominion: An Economic Commentary on Deuteronomy*, 2nd ed. (Dallas, Georgia: Point Five Press, [1999] 2012), ch. 22.

havior does. He adopts the words of baseball coach Leo Durocher: "Nice guys finish last." This psalm teaches otherwise.

## Conclusion

Psalm 1 introduces a comprehensive body of wisdom which rests on this presupposition: personal righteousness produces positive sanctions, while personal unrighteousness produces negative sanctions. This psalm rests on a view of the universe in which ethics is primary. This is taught throughout the Bible. It is taught repeatedly in Psalms. Unfortunately, it is not taught by the modern church.

# A COMPREHENSIVE INHERITANCE

*I will declare the decree: the LORD hath said unto me, Thou art my Son; this day have I begotten thee. Ask of me, and I shall give thee the heathen for thine inheritance, and the uttermost parts of the earth for thy possession.*

PSALM 2:7–8

This is a messianic psalm. We could even say that it is *the* messianic psalm. Here we read: "this day have I begotten thee." This passage is quoted twice in the epistle to the Hebrews as applying to Jesus Christ.[1]

God speaks to the Messiah in this psalm. He says for Messiah to ask Him to give Him the heathen for His inheritance. He also promises Him the uttermost parts of the earth for His possession. This does not refer to the world beyond the grave. The psalmist speaks of the heathen as being present in the world. The theocentric issue here is inheritance.

## A. Eschatological Views

There are three main approaches to eschatology: the doctrine of last things. Each has its distinctive features. Each has a specific social theory.[2]

This passage makes things exegetically difficult for amillennialists. It is possible for both premillennialists and postmillennialists to

---

1. "For unto which of the angels said he at any time, Thou art my Son, this day have I begotten thee? And again, I will be to him a Father, and he shall be to me a Son?" (Heb. 1:5). "So also Christ glorified not himself to be made an high priest; but he that said unto him, Thou art my Son, to day have I begotten thee" (Heb. 5:5).

2. Gary North, *Millennialism and Social Theory* (Tyler, Texas: Institute for Christian Economics, 1990).

take this passage literally. The postmillennialist applies it to the final phase of the kingdom of God in history, in which the gospel of Jesus Christ spreads across the whole face of the earth. The premillennialist interprets it as an aspect of the millennial reign of Christ on earth prior to the final judgment.

The amillennialist cannot interpret this passage literally. This passage makes no sense in the context of the amillennialist hermeneutic. There can be no question that this psalm is talking about the worldwide dominion of Jesus Christ in history. This language does not refer to some kind of spiritual or emotional state of mind, in which Christians, who have little influence in history, and who may be under the oppression of heathen, somehow reinterpret their situation to mean that they are in a position of authority. The only way for the amillennialist to interpret this passage literally is for him to say that Jesus Christ never does bother to ask God for the heathen as His inheritance or ask for the uttermost parts of the earth as His possession. Somehow, Jesus is not interested in extending His kingdom to include dominion over the heathen and possession of the uttermost parts of the earth. This makes even less sense than the amillennialist tradition of interpreting all biblical prophetic language of cultural victory as applying only to the psychological feelings of oppressed and culturally impotent Christians.

### B. Inheritance

In Psalms, we have promises of inheritance. Covenant-keepers are told that they will inherit the earth in history.[3] *The psalms do not refer to the world beyond the grave.* The Old Testament does not speak of exercising dominion after the resurrection. There are only a few Old Testament passages relating to the bodily resurrection,[4] and they do not speak of dominion.

This psalm goes on to say that the Messiah will break His enemies with a rod of iron. He will break them in pieces like a potter's vessel. I know of no hermeneutic that does not interpret these words as symbolic. When the Bible speaks of a rod of iron, it does not mean a literal rod of iron. When it speaks of bashing people to pieces, it does not mean literal pieces of people scattered around the ground. It does not mean frozen corpses hacked into solid pieces by a literal rod of iron. It refers to political and judicial dominion. It refers to the

3. Psalms 37:9, 11, 22, 29, 34; 82:11.
4. Job 14:14–15; Psalm 49:15; Isaiah 26:19; Daniel 12:1–2, 13; Hosea 13:14.

dominion exercised by a king over his realm. This is why the psalm goes on to say: "Be wise now therefore, all ye kings: be instructed, the judges of the earth" (v. 10). *This is judicial language*. It has to do with the civil covenant in history. The psalmist is not instructing the kings of the earth to join the church and thereby place themselves under the rule of elders. The Scriptures do not speak of elders as people who exercise dominion with a rod of iron. *This language refers to the civil covenant*.

The inheritance is economic. It encompasses the uttermost parts of the earth. It is a comprehensive inheritance. It is not simply a political inheritance; this inheritance is much wider than mere politics. The Messiah will inherit more than political office. The Bible teaches comprehensive redemption.[5] This redemption is the action of covenant- keepers who, as stewards of the Messiah, buy back (redeem) the whole world on behalf of the Messiah. It is the action of reclaiming every area of life in the name of Jesus Christ, by means of the Bible-revealed law of God, and by means of personal productivity. This redemption encompasses all three of the institutional covenants: church, family, and state.

### C. Representation

A king rules through subordinates. They represent him judicially in the civil courts. In economic affairs, the stewards of the king act as agents of the king, who build up the equity value of the king's domains. They report to the king, and the king evaluates the efficiency of their service. When this text speaks of the outermost parts of the earth as the possession of the Messiah, it is speaking of a system of representative government. This is not limited to civil government. It is government in the most comprehensive sense. It means to exercise dominion over the earth. This is what God requires of all mankind, as He revealed in Genesis 1:26–28. This is what I call the dominion covenant.[6] This covenant defines mankind. It preceded the four covenants: individual, church, family, and civil.

The psalmist says that when the Messiah asks God for His inheritance, He will be granted the outermost parts of the earth. Jesus declared after His resurrection that this messianic promise had been

---

5. Gary North, *Is the World Running Down? Crisis in the Christian Worldview* (Tyler, Texas: Institute for Christian Economics, 1988), Appendix C.

6. Gary North, *Sovereignty and Dominion: An Economic Commentary on Genesis* (Dallas, Georgia: Point Five Press, 2012), chaps. 3, 4.

fulfilled definitively in history. He said that all power had been given to Him, and that the disciples were to preach the gospel to all the earth (Matt. 28:18–20).[7] This is the Great Commission. It is comprehensive.[8] Jesus ratified His position as the Messiah by His affirmation of the fulfillment of this messianic promise. Through progressive sanctification and through evangelism, this psalm will be fulfilled in history.

The psalm closes with a promise: "Blessed are all they that put their trust in him." This is a positive sanction.

## Conclusion

This psalm announces the comprehensive rulership of the future Messiah. His inheritance is the uttermost parts of the earth. This means the whole world. The language is literal.

As with any monarch or estate owner, the Messiah rules through a system of hierarchy. His stewards represent Him judicially. They manage His estate on His behalf and for His benefit.

---

7. Gary North, *Priorities and Dominion: An Economic Commentary on Matthew*, 2nd ed. (Dallas, Georgia: Point Five Press, [2000] 2012), ch. 48.

8. Kenneth L. Gentry, *The Greatness of the Great Commission: The Christian Enterprise in a Fallen World* (Tyler, Texas: Institute for Christian Economics, 1990).

# 3

## ETHICS, NOT POWER

*What is man, that thou art mindful of him? and the son of man, that thou visitest him? For thou hast made him a little lower than the angels, and hast crowned him with glory and honour.*

PSALM 8:4–5

### A. Creation and Dominion

The theocentric issue here is hierarchy. This psalm begins with an affirmation of God's excellence. "O LORD our Lord, how excellent is thy name in all the earth! who hast set thy glory above the heavens" (v. 1). This places God high above the creation. His name is authoritative. He possesses authority over the enemy and the avenger (v. 2).

He possesses this authority because He is the Creator. The psalmist speaks of the heavens as the work of God's fingers (v. 3). This is obviously poetic language. It points to God as sovereign over the creation. God has ordained the moon and the stars (v. 3).

The psalmist then speaks of God as the creator of mankind. There was a purpose in His creation of mankind. God made man to have dominion over the works of His hands. God has put all things under mankind's feet. This is an aspect of the hierarchy of creation. While God is sovereign over the creation, He has delegated authority to that aspect of the creation made in His image: mankind. Mankind exercises God's authority over the creation. This is both judicial and economic authority.

The psalmist says that man exercises authority over sheep and oxen and beasts of the field (v. 7). He also exercises authority over the fowl of the air and the fish of the sea. This psalm reaffirms what

13

I have called the dominion covenant.[1] It was first revealed in Genesis 1:26–28. God specifically created mankind to exercise authority over the creation. The passage explicitly speaks about fish and the birds (v. 28).

Men do not directly exercise control over wild birds and fish in the sea. Men do not tell birds to fly this way or that. The authority that men exercise over birds and fish relates to *the authority of consumption*. Men have the right to kill birds and fish. Generally, this is done for food. Man's authority over these species is rarely done for training purposes. It is possible to train certain kinds of birds to perform tricks, and it is equally possible to train some large fish in the same way. But this is not what the psalmist is speaking about. He is talking about a general dominion, which is an affirmation of man's authority to use the birds of the air and the fish of the sea for his own purposes.

## B. Angels

The passage also speaks of angels. It says that God has placed mankind a little lower than the angels. He has crowned mankind with glory and honor.

This is a peculiar passage. It indicates that the angels are in some way superior to man. In what way? They are superior in terms of power, but this does not refer to dominion. God has not placed the birds of the air and the fish of the sea under the jurisdiction of angels. This is man's responsibility. So, if men are under angels, and they are also over the fish of the sea, do men represent angels? There is nothing in the Scriptures that indicates that this is the case. Men represent God to the creation, and they represent the creation to God. Man is the intermediary between God and the creation. Yet the text is explicit: man is a little lower than the angels.

Paul says in First Corinthians 6 that covenant-keepers will someday judge the angels. "Know ye not that we shall judge angels? how much more things that pertain to this life" (I Cor. 6:3)?[2] This indicates that, in terms of the *final judgment*, mankind will possess *authority over the angels*. But the psalmist indicates that men are under the angels. So, which is it? Does mankind possess authority over the angels, or do the angels possess authority over mankind?

---

1. Gary North, *Sovereignty and Dominion: An Economic Commentary on Genesis* (Dallas, Georgia: Point Five Press, 2012), chaps. 3, 4.

2. Gary North, *Judgment and Dominion: An Economic Commentary on First Corinthians*, 2nd ed. (Dallas, Georgia: Point Five Press, [2001] 2012), ch. 6.

If we consider the issue of power, the angels exercise authority over mankind. In the first chapter of the book of Job, we read of a debate between God and the fallen angel, Satan. God tells Satan that he has authority to inflict sickness or pain on Job. God restricts Satan from killing Job, but He does not restrict Satan from killing Job's children. All of them are then killed (vv. 18, 19).[3] Angels possess superior power to man.

This indicates that *the fundamental issue that divides mankind from the angels is ethics rather than power*. If it were a question simply of power, the angels would always win the confrontation. Yet there is no indication in the Bible that angels are at war with men physically. They occasionally exercise power, as we see in the New Testament's account of the demon that attacked the seven sons of Sceva (Acts 19:14–16). But the fundamental issues of life are ethical. They are not primarily matters of power. If the great debate between God and Satan were based simply on power, Satan would lose the conflict in every instance. So, the issues of life are primarily ethical. This is why God gave an ethical command to Adam regarding the forbidden fruit. It was not that Adam did not possess sufficient power to pick the fruit and eat it. It was that Adam was ethically prohibited from taking the fruit and eating it.

## Conclusion

The psalmist asks a question: Who is man? He answers this by reaffirming the account of God's creation week (Gen. 1). He presents man as lower than the angels, yet crowned with glory and honor. Man has authority over the birds and fishes. He is also ruler over "all things under his feet." This is comprehensive authority: earth, air, and water.

This authority is not based on man's power, for he possesses less power than the angels. Man's hierarchical authority is not based on power but on judicial authority. This is a matter of law, not power. It is a matter of the covenant: God's sovereignty, man's delegated authority, God's law, historical sanctions, and final judgment, in which covenant-keeping men will judge the angels.

---

3. Gary North, *Predictability and Dominion: An Economic Commentary on Job* (Dallas, Georgia: Point Five Press, 2012), ch. 1:B.

# 4

# DELIVERANCE OF THE POOR

*For the needy shall not alway be forgotten: the expectation of the poor shall not perish for ever.*

PSALM 9:18

## A. A Great Reversal

The theocentric issue here is God as the judge. This passage appears within the context of a psalm that deals with God's judgment against the wicked. In verse 9, we are told that the Lord "will be a refuge for the oppressed, a refuge in times of trouble." In verse 15, we read that "the heathen are sunk down in the pit that they made: in the net which they hid is their own foot taken." This is another way of saying that the evil which they had planned to impose on others snares them. *This is a reversal of fortune.* In verse 16, we read: "The Lord is known by the judgment which he executed: the wicked is snared in the work of his own hands." Again, the theme is a great reversal: the evil that men plan against others is the source of their own destruction. It is within this context that we read this verse: "For the needy shall not always be forgotten: the expectation of the poor shall not perish forever." The psalmist then declares: "Arise, O Lord; let not man prevail: let the heathen be judged in thy sight" (v. 19).

These passages deal with God's judgment. They are not primarily economic passages; they are judicial passages. The psalmist says that God rules over history. God rules in terms of the covenant, and every covenant has law and sanctions.[1] The psalmist says that those

---

1. Ray R. Sutton, *That You May Prosper: Dominion By Covenant*, 2nd ed. (Tyler, Texas: Institute for Christian Economics, [1987] 1992), chaps. 3, 4. Gary North, *Unconditional*

who are oppressed will be delivered at some point. There are limits to oppression. It is within the context of the theme of *deliverance from oppression* that he declares that the needy will not always be forgotten. He says that the expectation of a poor man will not perish forever. This does not mean that every needy person will eventually achieve middle-class status. The expectation of the poor man that someday he will escape his poverty may not be fulfilled. But the general expectation of deliverance for those people who are poor as a result of oppression by evildoers will at some point come to pass. *There will be a reversal of fortune.* Those who are oppressors will find that their oppression has turned upon them, and they will be destroyed.

## B. Oppression

The text does not say that people who were formerly poor will oppress their former oppressors. It says that God will destroy these oppressors. God does not authorize those who have been delivered from oppression to impose a new system of oppression. *The biblical concept of oppression is the misuse of civil law to deprive others of what should be lawfully theirs.*[2] God upholds legitimacy of His law. The psalmist is saying that those who oppress others will be snared by their own system and destroyed.

People in this passage are poor because of oppression. *Someone has misused the civil law in order to oppress them.* They are not poor as a result of their own incompetence. They are not poor because they lacked productivity. They are poor because they are the victims of evildoers.

The Bible does not teach that every poor individual will gain middle-class wealth or riches. It says only that at some point, *there will be widespread deliverance from judicial oppression.* If men are poor because they are oppressed by a corrupt legal order, they will at some point no longer be poor.

Nowhere in the Bible do we see a call for the civil government to impose a system of wealth redistribution from rich people in general to poor people in general. That would be a form of oppression: the use of the ballot box by the majority to extract wealth from a minority. This is exactly what the Bible prohibits. People are not to

*Surrender: God's Program for Victory*, 5th ed. (Powder Springs, Georgia: American Vision, 2010), chaps. 3, 4.

2. Gary North, *Authority and Dominion: An Economic Commentary on Exodus* (Dallas, Georgia: Point Five Press, 2012). Part 3, *Tools of Dominion* (1990), ch. 48.

oppress the poor by means of illegitimate legislation. *No group is to misuse the civil law in order to extract wealth from another group.*

### C. Psalm 10

Psalm 10 extends the message of Psalm 9. We read that wicked people persecute the poor. In Psalm 9, the psalmist writes that there will be a great reversal. The oppressor will find that his actions have led to his own destruction. This is a familiar theme throughout the Bible.[3] In Psalm 10, the psalmist says that the oppressors will be taken by their own devices. "The wicked in his pride doth persecute the poor: let them be taken in the devices that they have imagined" (v. 2). They have planned to oppress victims, but their schemes and dreams will blow up in their faces.

The wicked person is confident about his goals. He has great plans, the psalmist says. He boasts of his heart's desire (10:3). He blesses covetous people, yet covetous people are abhorred by God (10:3). In other words, he sees the world as a perverse mirror image of God's reality. What God criticizes, the wicked person praises. What God prohibits, the wicked person pursues.

In verse 10, the psalmist describes the evildoer. "In secret places, he murders innocent people. His eyes are set against the poor." This is a person who systematically violates biblical law. In verse 9, we read: "He lieth in wait secretly as a lion in his den: he lieth in wait to catch the poor: he doth catch the poor, when he draweth him into his net." This is a description of an individual who self-consciously breaks the Mosaic law. This is a classic oppressor.

The psalmist then calls on God to break the arm of the wicked person (10:15). This is a call for God to intervene in history and impose direct negative sanctions on men who systematically violate God's law in order to oppress the innocent. In Psalm 12, he writes: "For the oppression of the poor, for the sighing of the needy, now will I arise, saith the LORD; I will set him in safety from him that puffeth at him" (v. 5). There are historical sanctions. "The LORD shall cut off all flattering lips, and the tongue that speaketh proud things: Who have said, With our tongue will we prevail; our lips are our own: who is lord over us" (Psalm 12:3–4)?

---

3. Gary North, *Treasure and Dominion: An Economic Commentary on Luke*, 2nd ed. (Dallas, Georgia: Point Five Press, [2000] 2012), ch. 1.

## Conclusion

The psalmist announces that the oppressed poor will be delivered by God. The world is neither ethically random nor ethically perverse. It is governed by ethical cause and effect. The poor have legitimate hope that the oppressive judicial system will be removed by God at some point.

# 5

# OWNERSHIP: ORIGINAL AND DELEGATED

*The earth is the LORD's, and the fulness thereof; the world, and they that dwell therein.*

God owns the world

PSALM 24:1

This verse is the single most important verse in Christian economics. It is theocentric to the core. God owns the world.

## A. Original Ownership

Every economic theory has a concept of ownership. This is rarely stated at the beginning of an economics textbook. It is almost as if economists were deliberately concealing the fact that *the most fundamental principle of economic theory is the doctrine of ownership*.

Adam Smith began *The Wealth of Nations* (1776) with a discussion of the division of labor. He did not begin with the concept of private ownership. This left economic theory vulnerable to socialists and communists in the nineteenth century.[1] Because Smith did not begin his analysis with a theoretical defense of private property, socialists and communists had no difficulty in dealing with the concept of the division of labor from the point of view of state ownership of the means of production. There is nothing inherent in socialist production that is opposed to the concept of the division of labor. So, from a theoretical standpoint, Adam Smith left modern free market theory vulnerable, because he refused to deal systematically with the concept of ownership. It was not until the 1960s that free market economists began to develop a detailed theory of private ownership,

---

1. Tom Bethel, *The Noblest Triumph: Property and Prosperity Through the Ages* (New York: St. Martins, 1998), ch. 7.

despite the fact that their predecessors had built economic theory in terms of this concept.[2]

## B. Self-Ownership and Autonomy

Almost all free market economists begin with some variation of the theory of self-ownership. This concept rests on a doctrine of human autonomy. *There is no academic discipline that is more self-conscious in its affirmation of human autonomy than economics.*

Some economists believe that the economy is best established by means of the political order. We call these people socialists. Free market economists emphasize the importance of personal responsibility, and therefore they emphasize the benefits of the private ownership of the means of production. They argue that people are far more responsible over the administration of assets that they own, when compared to their administration of assets that they do not own.

### 1. Christian Economics

No system of humanist economics begins with the concept of God's ownership of all assets, including the means of production. Only Christian economics begins with this presupposition, and I know of no other economist other than myself who has begun his economic theory with this presupposition.[3]

This means that the reconstruction of economic theory to conform to biblical principles requires, above all, that economic theory begin with the presupposition, declared in Psalm 24:1, that God is the owner of all things. *God owns all things because He created all things. He owns all things because He is sovereign over all things.* He is responsible only to Himself. He answers to nobody, except when He wants to, as the book of Job affirms. This is the central message of the book of Job.[4]

The psalmist declares that God owns everything. When we combine this insight with the declaration of God in the first chapter of Genesis that man will exercise dominion over the creation (Gen. 1:27–28),[5] we encounter the biblical theory of *delegated ownership*.

---

2. *Ibid.*, ch. 20.

3. Gary North, *Inherit the Earth: Biblical Blueprints for Economics* (Ft. Worth, Texas: Dominion Press, 1987), ch. 1.

4. Gary North, *Predictability and Dominion: An Economic Commentary on Job* (Dallas, Georgia: Point Five Press, 2012).

5. Gary North, *Sovereignty and Dominion: An Economic Commentary on Genesis* (Dallas, Georgia: Point Five Press, 2012), ch. 4.

God is the primary owner; man is the secondary owner. God owns everything absolutely and comprehensively; man owns subordinately: point two of the biblical covenant model.[6] God establishes the terms of ownership. Man is required to adhere to these terms of ownership: point three of the biblical covenant model.[7]

This principle is most clearly displayed in the Bible's discussion of the Fall of man. God established boundaries around the tree of the knowledge of good and evil. He forbade man from eating from it. Any violation of this law was a violation of God's absolute property rights. So supreme were these property rights that God threatened to kill Adam if he transgressed this boundary. As it has turned out, God has sent the vast majority of individuals to hell, and will resurrect them only to deposit them in the lake of fire (Rev. 20:15), because *Adam and Eve violated God's property rights*. The Fall of man is presented in the Bible as a violation of property rights: eating from a forbidden tree that belonged exclusively to God.[8] This is how important the concept of property rights ought to be in theology. Yet theologians rarely discuss the Fall of man in terms of property rights.

God establishes a boundary around specific pieces of property, and He expects the boundary to be honored by non-owners. *Man's ownership is delegated ownership, not original ownership.* A man owns property only as a steward of God. He is responsible to God for the administration of this property. This is affirmed clearly in Jesus' parable of the property owner who delegates the administration of his property to three stewards, and then leaves on a long journey. He returns and requires an accounting of their administration of the property which he delegated to them (Matt. 25:14–30).[9]

## 2. Property Rights

Property rights are absolute with respect to God. They are not absolute with respect to anyone else. Therefore, the familiar defense of the free market by non-economists, namely, that private property rights are absolute, is erroneous. With the exception only of the fol-

6. Ray R. Sutton, *That You May Prosper: Dominion By Covenant*, 2nd ed. (Tyler, Texas: Institute for Christian Economics, [1987] 1992), ch. 2. Gary North, *Unconditional Surrender: God's Program for Victory*, 5th ed. (Powder Springs, Georgia: American Vision, [1980] 2010), ch. 2.

7. Sutton, ch. 3. North, ch. 3.

8. Gary North, *Sovereignty and Dominion: An Economic Commentary on Genesis* (Dallas, Georgia: Point Five Press, 2012), ch. 9.

9. Gary North, *Priorities and Dominion: An Economic Commentary on Matthew*, 2nd ed. (Dallas, Georgia: Point Five Press, [2000] 2012), ch. 47.

lowers of Murray Rothbard, modern economists do not speak of property rights as being absolute. They are defenders of the legitimacy of intervention by the state to establish the terms of ownership, exchange, and judicial arbitration. With the exception of anarchist economists, modern economists affirm the necessity of some intervention by an institution that is not established on the basis of the free market principle of high bid wins.

If Christian economists were consistent with what they say they believe about the authority of the Bible, they would go to Psalm 24:1 in search of the most fundamental of all economic principles: original ownership. If we do not know who is the owner of a piece of property, we are not in a position to enforce the law governing the administration of that piece of property. Property that is not owned is wasted. If owners do not purposefully administer their property, then the property will be wasted.

## 3. God's Autonomy

The crucial biblical concept of ownership is that the only autonomous agent in the universe is God. He sets His own law. He answers to no one. Therefore, *autonomy is an incommunicable attribute of God*. The common incommunicable attributes that are listed in systematic theologies are these: omniscience, omnipotence, and omnipresence. These are indeed incommunicable attributes. *But from the point of view of social theory, the most important incommunicable attribute of God is autonomy*. Once we understand this fundamental principle of theology, we are less likely to make the fundamental error of humanist economics and humanist social theory, namely, that mankind, either collectively or through individual ownership, possesses autonomy. This means that man does not establish the rules of ownership or anything else. Man is subordinate to God, and God lays down the rules. God has established the covenant with man, and the covenant takes precedence over voluntary contracts, or any other social arrangements, that individuals establish with each other.

## 4. Man's Ownership Is Hierarchical

The doctrine of God's sovereignty and absolute ownership leads to the doctrine of delegated ownership and stewardship. This means that *man's ownership is hierarchical*. It is fundamentally hierarchical. It is also horizontal, in the sense that individuals own specific pieces of property, and they make voluntary exchanges among each other.

Property ownership is not exclusively hierarchical, but it is fundamentally and originally hierarchical. This is why there has to be *a chain of command*, established by the civil government, in which the principle of the free market, namely, *high bid wins*, does not operate. The Bible makes it clear that the principle of high bid wins is not only illegitimate in the civil government, it is immoral. Any importation of the principle of high bid wins into civil government means that corruption is being substituted for justice. Bribery triumphs.

The concept of ownership is therefore grounded in the judicial category of the covenant. It is not grounded in the economic principle of efficiency. Efficiency is maximized in terms of a hierarchical judicial system that enforces property rights. *The civil judicial system is outside the system of private property rights.* The civil judicial system is a monopoly. It is not the outcome of competitive bidding in an open market. God has established a hierarchical system of property, meaning delegated ownership, which is enforced by a hierarchical system of sovereign civil courts. This was established in Exodus 18.[10]

There can be no exclusively horizontal ownership of property. Ownership is not a system in which autonomous individuals own pieces of property and exchange property with each other. There must always be an enforcement system, and the civil enforcement system relies on violence. *A system of exclusively horizontal ownership always leads towards a system of warlordism.* Those individuals who amass greater wealth then purchase armies, and they use these armies to gather even greater wealth. There is no escape from judicial hierarchy. There is no autonomous ownership for mankind.

## Conclusion

Psalm 24:1 announces the fundamental principle of Christian economics: *God owns everything*. Any attempt to build economic theory on any other concept of ownership leads to error. As Cornelius Van Til used to say, it does not matter how much you sharpen a crooked buzz saw, it will not cut straight. The precision of modern economic analysis does not cut straight.

---

10. Gary North, *Authority and Dominion: An Economic Commentary on Exodus* (Dallas, Georgia: Point Five Press, 2012), Part 1, *Representation and Dominion* (1985), ch. 19.

# 6

## A TRUSTWORTHY INHERITANCE

*The wicked borroweth, and payeth not again: but the righteous sheweth mercy, and giveth. For such as be blessed of him shall inherit the earth; and they that be cursed of him shall be cut off. The steps of a good man are ordered by the LORD: and he delighteth in his way. Though he fall, he shall not be utterly cast down: for the LORD upholdeth him with his hand. I have been young, and now am old; yet have I not seen the righteous forsaken, nor his seed begging bread. He is ever merciful, and lendeth; and his seed is blessed.*

PSALM 37:21–26

## A. Rival Views of Property

The theocentric issue here is the connection between ethics and inheritance. David contrasts the righteous and the wicked in terms of their attitude toward property. He says that the wicked person borrows but then refuses to repay. The righteous individual shows mercy by giving away resources. The wicked person is grasping. The righteous person is openhanded. The wicked person promises to repay as a way of gaining access to someone else's wealth. He then refuses to repay his debt, thereby becoming a thief. The righteous person not only does not ask to be repaid, he actually gives away wealth on the assumption that he will not be repaid.

The difference in attitude has to do with trust. The wicked person gains the trust of someone who lends him assets. He then refuses to repay the debt. He has violated the trust. He has used the other person's trust as a means of extracting wealth from him. In contrast, the generous person trusts God not to let him sink into poverty. Because he trusts God to repay, he feels confident that he can safely give away assets. The wicked person misuses the trust of the other person. The righteous person trusts God, knowing that God will not abandon him.

David says in the next verse that the blessed individual will inherit the earth. In contrast, the people whom God curses will be cut off. We see a parallel contrast. The wicked person misuses the trust of a generous person, or a least a person who has wealth to lend, and he attempts to cut off the generous person. He cuts off the person who trusted in him; God will in turn cut off this wicked borrower who refuses to repay. David contrasts this person with the righteous person, who trusts in God rather than the word of the person to whom he gives an asset. He trusts that God will repay him in history. He trusts in God, and therefore he has the courage to give away a portion of his wealth. Such a person, David says, will inherit the earth. In other words, he gives away a minimal amount of wealth, and he eventually inherits the earth. This is not about inheriting heaven—pie in the sky by and by. It is about inheriting wealth in this world.

David wrote these words a thousand years before the birth of Christ. People in his era who were generous did not inherit the earth. Then what is the meaning of the phrase? It means that the covenantal heirs of the righteous will, in the advanced phase of the millennial kingdom, inherit the earth. *There is a progressive transfer of wealth in history from covenant-breakers to covenant-keepers.* Over time, covenant-keepers prosper, and covenant-breakers do not. This is the cause-and-effect process that is described in Leviticus 26 and Deuteronomy 28.

## B. Righteousness and Risks

In the next passage, David says that the steps of a good man are ordered by the Lord (v. 23). The Lord delights in the way of a good man (v. 23). If a good man falls, he will not be cast down by God (v. 24). The Lord upholds him with his hand. This teaches that *the righteous individual has special protection from God*. It means that he can do righteously, including give away wealth, without risking destruction. God intervenes in history to take care of the righteous individual. God orders his steps.

David then makes a remarkable announcement. "I have been young, and now am old; yet have I not seen the righteous forsaken, nor his seed begging bread" (v. 25) David testifies that righteous people he has seen have never been reduced to such poverty that they had to beg bread. David lived in a time in which righteousness was more common than it was two centuries later in Israel and Judah. This was an era of prosperity for the nation, and it was an era of general righteousness. David, as the king, was representative of civil government generally. It was a righteous society, comparatively speaking, and so the righteous individual was in a position to be confident that God would protect him. He would not have to beg bread. Because of this, David says, the righteous person is ever merciful, and he lends money or assets to the poor. His seed is blessed by God. Notice that the positive sanctions are part of an inheritance.

David is testifying to the existence of an ethical cause-and-effect process that governed the social order of Israel. God upholds a righteous man. This gives confidence to the righteous man that he can safely give away his wealth. David says that he will inherit the earth. This means that in the covenant line, over time, the heirs of covenant-keepers will inherit the earth. *This is a uniquely postmillennial concept.* It is repeated often in this psalm.[1] It testifies to the existence of positive sanctions for covenant-keeping in history. It testifies also to negative sanctions for covenant-breaking in history.

This passage reinforces what Moses had told the Israelites just before the conquest of Canaan. Moses told them that covenant-keeping produces positive sanctions in history (Deut. 28:1–14). Covenant-breaking produces negative sanctions in history (Deut. 28:15–68). David reiterates this, not by appealing back to the words of Moses, but by testifying to what he has seen with his own eyes. God upholds the generous person. This serves as a down payment on the long-term system of inheritance which Moses taught to Israel, and which David reaffirms here. Covenant-keepers will inherit the earth.

### C. Cutting Off the Wicked

The disinheritance of the wicked is as sure as the inheritance of the righteous. "For the LORD loveth judgment, and forsaketh not his saints; they are preserved for ever: but the seed of the wicked shall be cut off" (v. 28). It is not just that the biological seed will be cut off. The inheritance will be cut off. *The inheritance of evildoers is transferred to covenant-keepers.* "The righteous shall inherit the land, and dwell therein for ever" (v. 29). The link between seed and land under the Mosaic law was tight. This had to do with the messianic promise given by Jacob. "The sceptre shall not depart from Judah, nor

---

1. Verses 9, 11, 22, 29, and 34.

a lawgiver from between his feet, until Shiloh come; and unto him shall the gathering of the people be" (Gen. 49:10). The basis of this inheritance is covenant-keeping—ultimately, the representative covenant-keeping of Jesus Christ.

> Wait on the LORD, and keep his way, and he shall exalt thee to inherit the land: when the wicked are cut off, thou shalt see it. I have seen the wicked in great power, and spreading himself like a green bay tree. Yet he passed away, and, lo, he was not: yea, I sought him, but he could not be found (vv. 34–36).

For a time, wickedness prospers. It grows in influence. It appears to be dominant. This does not last. "But the transgressors shall be destroyed together: the end of the wicked shall be cut off" (v. 38).

This is consistent with Leviticus 26 and Deuteronomy 28.

### Conclusion

David distinguishes wicked men from righteous men by means of their attitude toward wealth. The wicked man trusts wealth so much that he betrays his own trust. He borrows but does not repay. He undermines his reputation. In contrast is the righteous man who trusts God to uphold him. His trust is so great that he gives away wealth.

David testifies that he has personally seen the outcome of righteousness. He has not seen the righteous forsaken, nor his children begging bread. The generous inherit the earth. The wicked are cut off.

# 7

## AN UNCERTAIN INHERITANCE

*Surely every man walketh in a vain shew: surely they are disquieted in vain: he heapeth up riches, and knoweth not who shall gather them.*

PSALM 39:6

This is a universal condemnation. Everyone is subject to this. Men live their lives in a vain show. The translators used this phrase rather than *image*, which is how it usually is translated.[1] He is saying that *we live our lives as images*. Of course, we live as images of God, but we try to create our own public images. This is a form of public relations.

### A. Who Will Inherit?

The theocentric issue here is inheritance. David is concerned about the long-term effects of the wealth that he accumulates. He attributes to others the problem that he faces personally. He speaks of other people as building up riches, but without knowledge regarding who will inherit these riches. This same theme can be found in the Book of Ecclesiastes.

> Yea, I hated all my labour which I had taken under the sun: because I should leave it unto the man that shall be after me. And who knoweth whether he shall be a wise man or a fool? yet shall he have rule over all my labour wherein I have laboured, and wherein I have shewed myself wise under the sun. This is also vanity. Therefore I went about to cause my heart to despair of all the labour which I took under the sun (Eccl. 2:18–20).[2]

---

1. Genesis 1:26; 5:3; I Samuel 6:5, 11; II Kings 11:18.
2. Gary North, *Autonomy and Stagnation: An Economic Commentary on Ecclesiastes* (Dallas, Georgia: Point Five Press, 2012), ch. 4.

This is always a major problem with accumulated wealth. This wealth may survive the death of the person who accumulated it. A rich person wants to believe that the influence he establishes in history will be continued through his accumulated wealth. The problem he faces is this: he will not be in a position to administer this wealth. *Wealth is a tool of production, but the producer will eventually lose control over it.* At that point, his influence may be continued by others, or it may be re-directed. The tool of great wealth can be put to many uses. It can be put to many ends. A dead man has no control over the uses or ends to which his wealth will be put.

This problem is related to the fifth point of the biblical covenant: inheritance. It is the problem of succession.[3] An individual builds wealth in terms of a particular set of values (point three)[4] and a particular set of skills. He builds this wealth in terms of the prevailing opinions and standards that exist during his lifetime. But these standards can and do change over time. Those who inherit his wealth will face decisions of how to put this wealth to some use. They will have to decide which values should govern the administration of this accumulated wealth. This is the issue of rendering judgment: point four.[5]

The problem of succession faces every successful individual and organization. It is built into the creation. This is why the biblical covenant addresses the problem. From the moment that death entered the world, the problem of succession became one of the central problems of everyone's existence.

Wealth involves personal responsibility. We build up wealth in many forms during our lifetime. We are commanded by God to subdue the earth on His behalf (Gen. 1:27–28).[6] This requires that we accumulate wealth in one form or another. This wealth may be in terms of books written, organizations launched, students trained, and all the other aspects of what we call a legacy. The same problem faces every person who leaves behind a legacy. He does not know who will inherit this legacy.

A father may believe that his sons will administer his wealth in a particular way, according to a particular set of values. But he has no

---

3. Ray R. Sutton, *That You May Prosper: Dominion By Covenant*, 2nd ed. (Tyler, Texas: Institute for Christian Economics, [1987] 1992), ch. 5. Gary North, *Unconditional Surrender: God's Program For Victory*, 5th ed. (Powder Springs, Georgia: American Vision, [1987] 2010), ch. 5.

4. Sutton, ch. 5. North, ch. 3.

5. Sutton, ch. 4. North, ch. 4.

6. Gary North, *Sovereignty and Dominion: An Economic Commentary on Genesis* (Dallas, Georgia: Point Five Press, 2012), ch. 4.

guarantee that he has not been deceived by one or all of his sons. Also, as we know from the parable of the prodigal son, a son may rebel against his father.[7] This can take place during a father's lifetime, but it can also take place after the father has died. The heirs may be skilled deceivers.

Alternatively, once they receive the inheritance, they may go through a fundamental change in their thinking. Great wealth transfers great opportunities, and great opportunities always involve great responsibilities. Some people do not want the responsibilities, but they thoroughly enjoy the opportunities. This is why inheritances can get squandered by the heirs within a few years. The stories of such squandering are common. They are certainly more common than the stories of families that have maintained enormous wealth through several generations.

The supreme goal *of* history is the extension of the kingdom of God *in* history. This requires compound growth. The biblical concept of kingdom expansion is one of *conquest through service*. One kingdom grows at the expense of the other. This is why Jesus spoke of the kingdom of heaven as being like a mustard seed or leaven (Matt. 13:31–33).[8] It grows in influence.

## B. Confession of Faith

Maintaining the same confession, meaning the same view of life, is very difficult inter-generationally. One child who rebels against the confession of the founder of the legacy can deflect succeeding generations' commitment to those principles. *It is easy to break the chain. It is not easy to re-establish the chain.* This is why Jesus established His church. The institutional church maintains the original confession down through the generations. The institutional church is more committed to the transmission of the legacy than the family is or the civil government is. The church historically has been more successful in maintaining the original confession of the Founder than either the family or the state.

This is why *maintaining the confession of faith is more important than maintaining the accumulated wealth*. A man's first responsibility is to

---

7. The parable was about two sons who rebelled. One of them repented: the prodigal (Luke 15:11–32). Gary North, *Treasure and Dominion: An Economic Commentary on Luke*, 2nd ed. (Dallas, Georgia: Point Five Press, [2000] 2012), ch. 37.

8. Gary North, *Priorities and Dominion: An Economic Commentary on Matthew*, 2nd ed. (Dallas, Georgia: Point Five Press, [2000] 2012), ch. 30.

train up his children in the way they should go, so that they will not depart from it in their old age (Prov. 22:6). This is another way of saying that they will not depart from it after the death of their father. They will put whatever inheritance they received from him to effective use in terms of his confession.

A man rarely lives long enough to see his great-grandchildren grow to young adults. They are toddlers who have not embraced a confession of faith. A good man leaves a legacy to his children's children, but he is incapable of leaving the confession that enables him to extend his legacy when it comes to the lives of his great-grandchildren. He may keep a journal for them to read. Journals are written on paper that can last physically, but they are easily lost and easily ignored. He may record his ideas on digital media, but there is no way that an image on a screen or waves on a digital audio file can assure the founder of a dynasty that his legacy will be maintained by his children's grandchildren.

*Time replaces the dead.* It covers them up the way that dirt covers up a casket in a grave. Western Christendom once had a ceremony at the graveside.[9] Someone—maybe several people—would shovel dirt onto the casket. The symbol of this covering up is a good one. It reminds us that *most of what we do in life is covered up.* We are not much responsible for the distant consequences of our legacy, because we have virtually no authority over those consequences. Responsibility is associated with authority. When authority declines, responsibility declines.

This is why accumulated wealth in any form is such an enormous responsibility for the person who accumulates it. If he is successful in maintaining his wealth, he must transfer it to others, who will put it to use after he has departed from the scene. The responsibility of entrusting such a legacy is very great. The stories of rich men who establish charitable foundations, which are then captured by their ideological enemies, are common.

This psalm reminds men of their mortality. It reminds them that, no matter how much they achieve during their lifetimes, they will exercise no direct postmortem authority over the outcome of their efforts. It reminds them that if they see themselves as solely responsi-

---

9. The early New England Puritans did not have formal funerals, except a call to the cemetery, where the corpse was interred without ceremony. This began to change in the mid-seventeenth century. A funeral was held at the church, not at the graveside. Bruce Collin Daniels, *Puritans at Play: Leisure and Recreation in Puritan New England* (New York: Macmillan, 1995), p. 87.

ble for accumulating their wealth and transmitting their wealth, they are flying blind. They should retain confidence in God to administer the wealth left behind. They should have confidence in point two of the biblical covenant: hierarchy.[10] In economic terms, they must have confidence in God as the owner of all wealth, and the Person in charge of transferring this wealth to stewards who will act on His behalf. If a man has no confidence in the sovereignty of God and the commitment of God to the kingdom of God by means of the system of stewardship established by the dominion covenant, he places too much responsibility on his own shoulders. He thereby asserts autonomous responsibility for the administration of his wealth long after his death.

### Conclusion

This psalm reminds a man that he has little responsibility beyond his death, because he has almost no information about how or what the heirs will do with his legacy. So, a person who wants to extend his legacy through history in a way that benefits people in the future must come to grips with the fact that he is incapable of doing this alone with any degree of success. *Presumed autonomy ends with death*. He must face the limitations of his own mortality, and he must then strive to place his wealth in the hands of stewards who will administer this wealth on behalf of the confession of faith which enabled him to build this wealth. This is delegation. This is what God does with men. Men should do the same.

This psalm also reminds us that we are not very good stewards in our own lifetimes. We are nearly helpless in establishing the purposes to which our legacies will be put. The proper use of our legacies forces us to consider *the sovereignty of God in the hierarchy of all covenants*. It forces us to come to grips with *the covenantal nature of reality*. If we are unwilling to conform ourselves to God and His covenants, we will live under the curse of our inability to exercise control over the wealth which we accumulate. Presumed autonomy is self-destructive.

---

10. Sutton, *That You May Prosper,* ch. 2. North, *Unconditional Surrender*, ch. 2.

# BELOW-MARKET PRICING

*Thou sellest thy people for nought, and dost not increase thy wealth by their price.*

PSALM 44:12

One of the fundamental assumptions of free market economic theory is that individuals enter into voluntary transactions only when each of the parties believes that he will better himself by completing the transaction. If either party does not believe that the exchange will benefit him, he will not enter into the exchange.

## A. God's Negative Sanctions

The theocentric issue here is God as judge. In this verse, the psalmist tells God what God has been doing. This psalm contains a long list of negative sanctions that God has been imposing on the nation of Israel. It begins with a list of benefits that God had granted to Israel during the era of the conquest under Joshua. The psalmist sees God as the source of positive corporate sanctions as well as negative.

One of the negative sanctions that the psalmist lists is that God has sold His people without seeking a profit. This means that God has acted against the interests of those who are sold into servitude, yet He does not make a profit on the transaction.

From the point of view of free market economic theory, such a transaction is economically irrational. No one knowingly enters into a transaction in which he sells an asset for less than the asset is worth in a competitive market. To sell an asset for less than the asset is worth is to indulge in a form of charity. The seller of the asset is transferring wealth to the buyer, yet the seller does not insist on compensation comparable to the value of the asset being transferred.

From an economic standpoint, such a transaction makes no sense. The psalmist nevertheless announces that this is what God has done. He does not say exactly how that God has sold His people. The implication is that God owns them, and that He has sold them to a high-bidding purchaser. Someone has purchased all of the servants whom God has put up for exchange. The psalmist does not say who this individual is. The implication is that Israel has been suffering from various forms of tyranny. God has arranged for Israel to suffer this tyranny. The meaning of being sold into servitude is that an individual loses authority over himself and his household. This authority is transferred to the purchaser of a servant.

The psalmist indicates that this is a form of judgment on the nation of Israel. The fact that God would sell His people without seeking to make a profit is indicative of the anger of God against the actions of Israelites. This is not a strictly economic transaction. As a strictly economic transaction, the sale of servants at no profit to the seller makes no sense. So, the psalmist is making a covenantal point. He is arguing that point four of the biblical covenant, sanctions,[1] is being upheld by God. God upholds the fourth point of the biblical covenant by selling His people into servitude. He refuses to intervene in order to deliver his people from bondage. He could have intervened, but He has not.

This psalm indicates that *God is bringing covenantal judgment against the nation of Israel.* It acknowledges that God is completely in control. It is an affirmation of God's sovereign action in history. This psalm therefore constitutes a covenant lawsuit. It is a warning, not to God, but to the hearers and readers of the psalm: the events that had taken place in Israel are not random. They were the outcome of God's enforcement of His covenantal law by means of covenantal sanctions. In this case, the sanctions are negative, because the sin of the nation is overt. The psalmist is not issuing some kind of covenant lawsuit against God. We must therefore view his complaints against God as a covenant lawsuit against the nation of Israel. He acknowledges that bad times have come, but he attributes these bad times to the systematic intervention of God into the society. He understands that it is God who has intervened on behalf of His law. The events are not random.

---

1. Ray R. Sutton, *That You May Prosper: Dominion By Covenant*, 2nd ed. (Tyler, Texas: Institute for Christian Economics, [1987] 1992), ch. 4. Gary North, *Unconditional Surrender: God's Program for Victory*, 5th ed. (Powder Springs, Georgia: Point Five Press, 2012), ch. 4.

The psalm is indirectly a call for national repentance. It is presented in the form of a complaint against God, but it was written in order to persuade covenant-keepers that they should abandon their covenant-breaking practices and go back to the Mosaic law. The psalmist insists that Israel has not apostatized. The nation is still full of covenant-keepers.

> All this is come upon us; yet have we not forgotten thee, neither have we dealt falsely in thy covenant. Our heart is not turned back, neither have our steps declined from thy way; Though thou hast sore broken us in the place of dragons, and covered us with the shadow of death. If we have forgotten the name of our God, or stretched out our hands to a strange god; Shall not God search this out? for he knoweth the secrets of the heart. Yea, for thy sake are we killed all the day long; we are counted as sheep for the slaughter. Awake, why sleepest thou, O Lord? arise, cast us not off for ever (vv. 17–23).

The psalmist is presenting a legal case for Israel. He calls on God to relent. The people have learned their lesson. God can conscientiously remove His curses. "For our soul is bowed down to the dust: our belly cleaveth unto the earth. Arise for our help, and redeem us for thy mercies' sake" (vv. 25–26). The nation has not earned God's favor through righteousness, but instead relies on God's grace.

### B. Amos' Covenant Lawsuit

Over three centuries later, Amos indirectly invoked the psalmist's words. He applied them to covenant-breakers. "Thus saith the LORD; For three transgressions of Israel, and for four, I will not turn away the punishment thereof; because they sold the righteous for silver, and the poor for a pair of shoes" (Amos 2:6). The Hebrew word indicates that the shoes in this case were sandals. Silver was worth having, but a pair of sandals were surely not worth what a human being was worth. Why would anyone who owned a Hebrew servant sell him for a pair of sandals? This makes no sense economically.

The next verse throws additional light on the practice. Example: "That pant after the dust of the earth on the head of the poor, and turn aside the way of the meek" (Amos 2:7a). The Hebrew word translated here as "pant" is elsewhere translated as "swallow." "Whose harvest the hungry eateth up, and taketh it even out of the thorns, and the robber swalloweth up their substance" (Job 5:5). It is also translated as "devour." "I have long time holden my peace; I have been still, and refrained myself: now will I cry like a travailing woman; I will destroy and devour at once" (Isa. 42:14). The sellers were driven by perversity: the enjoyment of destruction. They wanted to destroy poor people, heaping dust on the heads of the poor. So, they sold them cheap, out of spite. So corrupt had men become that they did not care what price they received. They sold their victims because they enjoyed demonstrating their ability to oppress others. To oppress those who were poor and meek had become a great source of social status for people with wealth and political influence.

We say that "price is no consideration." We mean that a high price is not a major barrier to a purchase. Amos was saying that human freedom was held in such low esteem by the sellers that any price was acceptable. They were walking away from money. They could get silver, but some of them sold their brethren for sandals. This was what the leftist American economist Thorstein Veblen called conspicuous consumption.[2] As in imperial Rome, when rich men—and Cleopatra—would publicly drop a ground-up pearl into a cup of wine and then drink the wine, so were the Israelite oppressors.

This must have been very profitable for those entrepreneurs who were engaged in the domestic slave trade, buying for sandals and selling for silver. But these sales could not have been easily predictable by slave traders. The sales must have been random. Two organized markets cannot have significant price differences for essentially the same product if free trade is allowed by the civil magistrates. Entrepreneurs will buy in one market, raising prices, and sell in the other, lowering prices. Prices will tend to equalize.

If we take Amos' words literally, the sale of Hebrew slaves in Israel and Judah was not a quest for financial profit. It was a quest for status: conspicuous consumption. It was *status through oppression*. This indicated the extent of the moral decline and judicial corruption.

Amos accused lawless Israelites of doing what the psalmist says here that God has been doing. Amos condemned rich Israelites who sold slaves for a pittance. The implication of this prophetic message is that the sellers were acting in terms of rebellious attitudes. They were not trying to seek a profit; they were simply showing their authority over the lives of other men and women. They sold property, not to the highest bidder, but to anyone who wanted to buy the services of slaves. It was an assertion of wealth. It was a way to show

---

2. Thorstein Veblen, *The Theory of the Leisure Class: An Economic Study of Institutions* (New York: Macmillan, [1899] 1902), ch. 4.

other people that money does not matter.[3] Yet this is the implication of what the psalmist asserts regarding the practice of God. God has sold His servants without seeking a profit. This is not because God is evil; it is because God upholds the terms of His covenant with Israel. He demonstrates that He is beyond the need to make a profit. He is sovereign. This is the same sort of statement that was made by covenant-breakers in Israel centuries later. They were also asserting that they were sovereign. They were also showing that money did not matter to them. But this attitude on the part of covenant-breakers is illegitimate. This was the message of Amos.

## Conclusion

The psalmist acts as Israel's defense attorney in God's court. God has begun to apply the negative sanctions of His national covenant. The psalmist acknowledges God's actions. He then argues that the nation has not departed from God entirely. There are still covenant- keepers who honor God. He calls on God to show grace.

He argues that God is losing money from the imposition of negative sanctions. "Thou sellest thy people for nought, and dost not increase thy wealth by their price." Why keep doing this? He is asking: "What is in it for you?" Why not remove these sanctions? "All this is come upon us; yet have we not forgotten thee, neither have we dealt falsely in thy covenant" (v. 17). Economically, this makes no sense. Covenantally, it does. But the national covenant has not been completely broken. So, please withhold correction, the psalmist asks God.

---

3. Gary North, *Restoration and Dominion: An Economic Commentary on the Prophets* (Dallas, Georgia: Point Five Press, 2012), ch. 28.

# 9

# THE FUTILITY OF RICHES

*Wherefore should I fear in the days of evil, when the iniquity of my heels shall compass me about? They that trust in their wealth, and boast themselves in the multitude of their riches; None of them can by any means redeem his brother, nor give to God a ransom for him.*

PSALM 49:5-7

The theocentric issue here is God's sanctions. These words introduce the most detailed discussion of economics that is found in the Book of Psalms. It begins with a description of negative sanctions, "when the iniquity of my heels shall compass me about." This is a strange passage. What is the meaning of "heel"? It appears to be from the same root as the word for someone who lies in wait to capture a person. "And when they had set the people, even all the host that was on the north of the city, and their **liers in wait** on the west of the city, Joshua went that night into the midst of the valley" (Josh. 8:13).

## A. Fear and Trust

The psalmist asks a rhetorical question: "Wherefore should I fear in the days of evil?" He is under attack, yet he says that he should not fear this. Why not? To answer this, he moves to a consideration of someone who trusts in riches, who boasts in the multitude of his riches. In the time of crisis, riches will not help those who possess them.

He says that rich men will not be able to redeem a brother, meaning a close relative. A rich man will not be able to give God a ransom for this relative. In such a time as this, the psalmist says, earthly riches count for nothing. An individual who boasts of his wealth in good times will find that his wealth does him no good in a time of extreme crisis.

The language of the two verses that follow indicates that the psalmist is talking about redemption from physical death. "(For the redemption of their soul is precious, and it ceaseth for ever:) That he should still live for ever, and not see corruption" (vv. 8–9). When he speaks of "the redemption of their soul," he is not talking about eternal life in the sense of deliverance from the final judgment. He is talking about deliverance from the threat of imminent physical death. No one can escape physical death. No one lives forever, physically speaking, never to see corruption. That promise—not seeing corruption—is a messianic promise. "For thou wilt not leave my soul in hell; neither wilt thou suffer thine Holy One to see corruption" (Psalm 16:10). Peter cited this passage in Acts 2, preaching to the Jews. He said that it was fulfilled by Jesus. Even in this case, Jesus Christ, the Messiah, did taste physical death. He escaped bodily corruption, because of the resurrection and the ascension, but he did not escape death. He paid God's ransom to God.

## B. Physical Death

Here, the psalmist begins a description of the effects of physical death. This raises the issue of inheritance. He says that wise men die, and so do fools and brutish people (v. 10). Wise men leave their wealth to others. Every man hopes that his house, meaning the legacy of the household he established, will continue forever. He hopes that his influence and memory will extend to all generations. Men of great wealth or power even name their estates after themselves. The psalmist is making the point that no one escapes death, no house survives forever, no family name survives forever, and land is eventually re-named after someone else. All land will eventually fall into a conqueror's hand. So, men who put their faith in the long-term impact of whatever it is that they leave behind are placing their trust in a vapor. Such trust is hopeless.

He goes so far as to say that a man who dies is like an animal that dies. There is no legacy of the animal, and there is no legacy of the individual. This does not mean that there is in fact no legacy whatso-

---

1. "Because thou wilt not leave my soul in hell, neither wilt thou suffer thine Holy One to see corruption" (Acts 2:27). "He seeing this before spake of the resurrection of Christ, that his soul was not left in hell, neither his flesh did see corruption. This Jesus hath God raised up, whereof we all are witnesses" (Acts 2:31–32).

ever. A man is not an animal. The psalmist is making a comparison. Man is more like an animal with respect to the survival of his legacy than he is to an immortal creature whose reign extends down through history. The common burden of physical death strikes the wise man and the fool, the rich man and the brute. This common legacy of all men undermines the differences between the legacies between a rich man and a poor man, between a wise man and a fool. Most legacies eventually are severed from people's memory about the founders. Through many sons and daughters, through many generations, the heirs' memories of the founders fade. Those people who trust in wealth to sustain their memory in history ignore what should be obvious: *future generations forget*.[2]

He says that an individual's body is laid in a grave. This is the equivalent of an animal that is laid in the grave. He has a memorable phrase: "The upright will have dominion over them in the morning" (v. 14). This is an affirmation of the covenantal basis of dominion. The upright individual will exercise dominion on the day after the death of the person who puts trust in riches. The indication here is that the *inheritance is covenantal*. It is based on covenantal conformity to the Bible-revealed laws of God. The individual who trusts in God, and who obeys the laws of God, is a righteous person. This person will have dominion over the legacy of those who trusted in riches. The Book of Proverbs reasserts this emphatically. "The wealth of the sinner is laid up for the just" (Prov. 13:22b).[3]

The psalmist says that God will redeem his soul from the power of the grave. When death threatens, God will intervene and deliver him from the calamity that faces him. This is what he said at the beginning of this passage. He is not saying that he will somehow live forever, never tasting physical death. He is saying only that the individual who trusts in God is in a position to have confidence that God will deliver him. The individual who trusts in riches to deliver him is resting on a broken reed (Isa. 36:6).

The psalmist then tells the listener not to be afraid when someone else is made rich. The glory of that person's house is increased. This is a short-term phenomenon, for when he dies, "he shall carry nothing away: his glory shall not descend after him" (v. 17). This theme is

---

2. Even with the Word Wide Web, with its seemingly permanent digital communications technologies, memories will fade. There will be too many forefathers for the descendants to study. Any short YouTube videos will not convey much information.

3. Gary North, *Wisdom and Dominion: An Economic Commentary on Proverbs* (Dallas, Georgia: Point Five Press, [2007] 2012), ch. 41.

found throughout the Bible. Every individual dies physically. He is not capable of taking any of his earthly possessions to a world beyond the grave. His glorious achievements in history will in no way benefit him. During his lifetime, the psalmist says, he blessed his own soul. Men praised him. But he will go to the generation of his fathers. He will go into the grave. An individual who does not understand this in the days of his own glory, in the days when other men praise him, is like the beasts that perish (v. 20). Such an individual is as ignorant as a beast. He does not understand the temporary nature of his riches, his power, and his fame.

### C. Mammon

The psalmist is talking about a major disaster that overtakes a man. His point is that men who trust in riches under such circumstances will find that they have put their trust in a false god. In contrast, he says that the individual who trusts in God will be delivered.

This is an early declaration of the truth that Jesus announced: a man cannot serve two gods, meaning God and Mammon (Matt. 6:24).[4] He must choose one of these to serve faithfully. It is impossible to serve them both faithfully. Mammon is the immanent god who promises more in history for his followers. The God of the Bible promises to deliver those who are committed to Him covenantally, meaning those who work to extend His kingdom in history. Mammon tells believers that they can accumulate wealth, power, fame, and honor mostly by their own efforts.

God tells His followers that history has limits, and that only to the extent that people are committed to God and the extension of His kingdom will they achieve their goal: a memorable legacy. The psalmist does not say that God guarantees that an individual will be remembered by future generations. On the contrary, he says precisely the opposite. The implication is that God will remember, and this is the only memory that counts.

### Conclusion

Here is the psalmist's message: everything that an individual accumulates for himself and his family in history will dissipate in history. Everything that an individual on his own authority attempts to do to

---

4. Gary North, *Priorities and Dominion: An Economic Commentary on Matthew*, 2nd ed. (Dallas, Georgia: Point Five Press, [2000] 2012), ch. 14.

guarantee his memory down through the generations will fail. Anyone who believes that he can achieve such immortality through future memories is like a beast. The beast has no comprehension of the way the world works. Neither does the individual who trusts in the work of his own hands to achieve for himself a legacy of honor and fame in history.

# 10

# ORIGINAL OWNERSHIP

*For every beast of the forest is mine, and the cattle upon a thousand hills.*

Here, in a memorable phrase, is the biblical concept of God's original ownership. *There is no more fundamental doctrine for Christian economic theory.* This verse is reinforced by Psalm 89:11: "The heavens are thine, the earth also is thine: as for the world and the fulness thereof, thou hast founded them." This verse ties the doctrine of God's original ownership to God's creation of the world. Christian economic theory must begin here: *creation and ownership.* Any attempt to begin with any other presupposition will inevitably lead into humanism or idolatry. It will place sovereignty somewhere other than in God.

## A. A Theocentric Universe

God is the center of the universe. God is primary; the universe is secondary. God is the Creator; the universe is created. This leads to a conclusion: *the universe is theocentric.* The Bible's account of God's relationship to the universe begins with God: "In the beginning God created the heaven and the earth" (Gen. 1:1).[1] The entire story of God's relationship with the universe is therefore theocentric. Biblical law is theocentric. Everything is theocentric.

*Christian economic theory is theocentric.* The Christian economist should therefore begin with the biblical doctrine of creation. The biblical doctrine of creation leads to an inevitable economic conclusion: *God owns the world.* This is not simply a logical conclusion; it is the

---

1. Gary North, *Sovereignty and Dominion: An Economic Commentary on Genesis* (Dallas, Georgia: Point Five Press, [1982] 2012), ch. 1.

44

explicit statement in this passage. Man does not own the cattle on a thousand hills: God owns them. God also owns the thousand hills.

This is why a Christian economist who is serious about defending economics as it really operates has a moral and intellectual obligation to begin his discussion of the way the world works economically with the Bible's doctrine of creation and the Bible's doctrine of God's primary ownership. *Primary ownership is exclusively God's ownership.* All other ownership is delegated. God delegates control over scarce economic resources to individuals and to individuals acting in collective associations. This is the economic application of the dominion covenant (Gen. 1:27–28).[2] This is the economic application of point two of the biblical covenant: hierarchy.[3]

### B. Adam Smith's Secondary Starting Points

Adam Smith is widely regarded as the founder of modern economics. This is not because he was the best economist of his day, or because he was the original thinker who created modern economic thought. Neither was the case.[4] He was the great popularizer, despite the fact that his economics book is over eight hundred pages.

*The Wealth of Nations* has two main ideas, which are introduced early in the book. The first idea is the division of labor (Chapter 1). Smith offers a discussion of a pin factory. He shows that by breaking down the tasks of creating a pin in such a way that a common laborer can master a particular task, a pin factory produces a much higher output of pins. This is a good insight, but it has almost no analytical application in the rest of the book. Also, a socialist economist can invoke the same doctrine of increased productivity through specialization of production and the division of labor. So, there is nothing uniquely free market in Adam Smith's use of the division of labor.

The second major concept of Smith's is that in order to persuade people to cooperate with you, you must offer them benefits. Smith begins with self-interest, but he extends the concept of self-interest to include service to others. In order to get what you want, you must

---

2. *Ibid.*, ch. 4.

3. Ray R. Sutton, *That You May Prosper: Dominion By Covenant*, 2nd ed. (Tyler, Texas: Institute for Christian Economics, [1987] 1992), ch. 2. Gary North, *Unconditional Surrender: God's Program for Victory*, 5th ed. (Powder Springs, Georgia: American Vision, [1980] 2010), ch. 2.

4. Murray Rothbard, *Economic Thought Before Adam Smith: An Austrian Perspective on the History of Economic Thought*, 2 vols. (Auburn Alabama: Mises Institute, [1995] 2006), I, ch. 16.

give someone else what he wants (Chapter 3). This is the most important concept in *The Wealth of Nations*. It is the methodological starting point for free market economics.

Smith devoted very little space in his book to the concept of private ownership. He did not discuss private ownership from a theoretical standpoint. He assumed private ownership, but he did not explain it. This set back free market economics by almost two centuries. It was not until the 1960s that free market economists began studying the concept of private property in terms of the analytical tools provided by economic logic. For 185 years, socialist economists had what amounted to a free ride.[5]

## C. No Self-Ownership

The psalmist does not begin with the doctrine of human autonomy. He does not begin with the doctrine of the autonomous human logic. He does not begin with a series of logically irrefutable axioms. He does not begin with a detailed historical study of cattle on hills. He begins with a declaration: God owns the cattle on a thousand hills. This does not mean that God does not own the cattle on hill number 1001. It means that God owns everything.

God alone possesses absolute rights of ownership. This means that all subordinate rights of ownership are limited. There is no absolute right of private ownership. There is no absolute right of anything when we are speaking of man's rights. *Man's rights are derived from God's extension of rights to him.* Man's rights are not attained on his own autonomy.

This means that *man has no absolute right of self-ownership.* The most prominent forms of libertarian economics begin with the assumption of the absolute right of self-ownership. There is no such absolute right. It is merely an assertion of the self-proclaimed autonomous man regarding his own autonomy. There is also no absolute right of state ownership. The great intellectual battle that has gone on between free market economists and socialist economists has been framed in terms of a falsehood: the autonomy of man and the autonomous rights of man. There is no such autonomy, and there are no such absolute rights.

The sovereignty of God is point one of the biblical covenant.[6] Its

---

5. Tom Bethel, *The Noblest Triumph: Property and Prosperity Through the Ages* (New York: St. Martins, 1998), ch. 20.

6. Sutton, *That You May Prosper*, ch. 1. North, *Unconditional Surrender*, ch. 1.

application in the field of economic theory is the absolute sovereignty of God over the creation. This means God's absolute rights of ownership over everything in the universe.

## D. Professional Isolation

Because a Christian economist should begin with the biblical doctrine of creation, which leads to the biblical doctrine of primary ownership by God, he should not begin with common-confession principles that are shared by most other economists, let alone the general public. *A Christian economist should start with the Bible.* By starting with the Bible, he cuts himself off from the vast majority of those people who call themselves economists. As he will discover soon enough, he also cuts himself off from the vast majority of people who call themselves Christians.

Most Christians have been trained in tax-funded government schools. They are deliberately trained to reason on this assumption: the God of the Bible is irrelevant to logic, history, science, politics, economics, and everything else that is part of the curriculum of the modern secular university. It is illegal in the United States for a teacher in a tax-supported educational institution to argue that the Bible is authoritative in any area of the curriculum. A Christian teacher in such an institution must spend his career teaching what he knows is a lie: that the God of the Bible and the revelation of the Bible are irrelevant to academic endeavors. If he does not believe that it is a lie, then he is self-deceived. He has been taken in by the deceivers who certified him academically.

Christian economists today refuse to begin with the doctrine of creation as stated in the first chapter of Genesis. They therefore refuse to begin with the concept of God's absolute ownership of everything. They refuse to discuss human ownership as God-delegated ownership: stewardship for the original Owner. They adopt the presuppositions of the humanist worldview. *They begin with autonomous man.* Free market economists begin with autonomous individual man. Socialist economists begin with autonomous collective man. Christian economists should not begin with the methodology offered by either tradition, but they do. They do not do this self-consciously. They do it after years of training. They can think no other way.

## Conclusion

The psalmist declares that God owns the cattle on a thousand hills. This is the first corollary of Christian economic theory. The first axiom is that God created the heaven and the earth.

The biblical doctrine of creation should be the starting point of Christian social theory. It has been my starting for all volumes in my *Economic Commentary on the Bible*.

# 11

## THE IRRELEVANCE OF STATUS

*Surely men of low degree are vanity, and men of high degree are a lie: to be laid in the balance, they are altogether lighter than vanity.*

PSALM 62:9

### A. Social Position

The theocentric issue here is God as the imputer of status. God is the judge. The psalmist tells us that men of low degree are vanity, and men of high degree are vanity. Weighed in the balance, they are all found to be lighter than vanity. The point he is making is This: *your social position is irrelevant if your confession of faith is false.* It is vanity. The low man on the totem pole is no better off than the high man on the totem pole.[1] Every position in the social hierarchy is equally irrelevant.

He then tells the would-be criminal not to trust in oppression or wealth. "Trust not in oppression, and become not vain in robbery: if riches increase, set not your heart upon them" (v. 10). Criminal behavior is hopeless.

The biblical meaning of oppression is narrowly defined. It refers to the misuse of civil government to extract wealth or other assets from someone who does not possess judicial authority.[2] Anyone who trusts in oppression trusts in something that is inherently untrustworthy. *Oppression is a form of state-approved robbery.* The psalmist also says that

---

1. A totem pole is a carved pole produced by American Indians in the Pacific Northwest of North America. The poles are associated with specific clans or families. The best-known style of totem poles has carved faces of demons, each face above the other.

2. Gary North, *Authority and Dominion: An Economic Commentary on Exodus* (Dallas, Georgia: 2012), Part 3, *Tools of Dominion* (1990), ch. 48.

robbery in general should not be relied on. What is the typical goal
for someone who relies on robbery? The accumulation of riches. The
psalmist then says not to trust in riches, either.

In verse 11, we read the following: "God hath spoken once; twice
have I heard this; that power belongeth unto God" (v. 11). God is in a
position to bring judgment against those who misuse power in order
to steal from others. The psalmist praises God as the source of mercy.
"For thou render rest to every man according to his work" (v. 12). This
is a warning to anyone who misuses power in order to steal from others. God is a judge, and He possesses the power to bring judgment
against those who violate His law. Anyone who is familiar with the Bible understands that God has laws against theft. The commandment
is: "Thou shalt not steal" (Ex. 20:15).[3]

## B. Status: Beyond Mere Money

What is unique about this psalm is its forthright dismissal of social
status. Most people spend their lives accumulating wealth in order
to rise in the eyes of their neighbors. They do not wish to be known
merely as having the ability to make money. They want to receive
the acceptance of people who are honored for something other than
money. Usually, the something other than money means membership
in a self-policed, closed group to which they alone belong. Usually,
access to high social status is based on the possession of old money.
Old money is money that is inherited through several generations.

It is a well-known fact of life that the sons and grandsons of rich
people tend to dissipate the inheritance. In medieval times, the way
that families kept this from happening, in order to preserve the family name, was to give the family's land to the oldest son. He was not
allowed to sell this land, except to pay off debts. The younger sons
received relatively little of the inheritance. This is opposed to the biblical principle of the double portion for the eldest son (Deut. 21:15–
17).[4] In contrast, the eldest son under the system of primogeniture
received virtually the whole of the inheritance. This preserved the
family name, but only by disinheriting younger sons who also possessed the family name.

Such a system of inheritance is expressly unbiblical. The eldest
son under the Mosaic covenant received a double portion. Why? Be-

---

3. *Ibid.*, ch. 28.
4. Gary North, *Inheritance and Dominion: An Economic Commentary on Deuteronomy*,
2nd ed. (Dallas, Georgia: Point Five Press, [1999] 2012), ch. 50.

cause he had double responsibilities for the care of his aged parents. The other sons were not cut off from the family inheritance. They were part of the inheritance because they bore the family's name. So, the effect of inheritance in a large Hebrew family was to dissipate the ownership of land especially, but also any other assets possessed by the family. The larger the family, the more the economic legacy was dissipated. This is the correct procedure. God does not want people to trust in an economic inheritance. *The primary inheritance is confessional and ethical.* This inheritance is the legacy of raising of children according to the word of God. It means passing down to them the same vision of the extension of the kingdom of God in history that the founder of the family fortune believed in. The family's primary legacy is therefore confessional and ethical.

Jesus warned against faith in Mammon (Matt. 6:24).[5] Mammon's confession of faith is this: "More for me in history." It is a popular confession. When men believe in Mammon more than they believe in God, they want to preserve a legacy that will be remembered. They want to be famous for having established a legacy in the first place. They seek a kind of immortality through the memory of future generations. The Psalms say elsewhere that this goal is an illusion (Psalm 39:6).[6] But men who believe in Mammon do not have a concept of history in which inheritance is the commitment to extend the kingdom of God, not to extend the kingdom of man. This is why Mammon offers a lie to his followers.

## C. Social Climbing

The person who seeks to escape from the social status of low degree desires to enter the social status of a higher degree. The psalmist says that both positions are equally irrelevant. They are equally lightweight. They are lightweight because they rest, not on the sovereignty of God, but on the supposed sovereignty of man.

A person who seeks high status by accumulated wealth may be tempted to oppress people or rob people. What matters to him is rising in social status, not the means by which he rises. Yet social status is always concerned with means as well as ends. If anything, the means are more important than the ends. It is not sufficient to possess great wealth in the quest to rise in social status. The heirs of

---

5. Gary North, *Priorities and Dominion: An Economic Commentary on Matthew*, 2nd ed. (Dallas, Georgia: Point Five Press, [2000] 2012), ch. 14.
6. Chapter 7.

those who long ago achieved great wealth do not want competition from newcomers who achieve great wealth. They do not want to be displaced by productive people who get rich by serving consumers. They want to maintain their high social status on the basis of characteristics other than making money. So, it is almost hopeless for a person to seeks to become someone of high degree to do so by accumulating great wealth.

*Social status is always imputed status.* Someone who possesses high social status imputes to another person those characteristics which he says, and those among his peers say, make a person eligible to enter the company of those who possess high social status. People lower on the totem pole also impute high status to those whom they perceive to be members of a closed elite far above them. But, in either case, it is men who make the imputation of status, and the psalmist has no faith in men. God alone renders relevant judgment, not man. God renders to every man according to his works (v. 12). His imputation of status is what matters, not the imputation made by those within a closed circle, an elite, or by those who are excluded from the closed circle. The judgment of man cannot be safely trusted. Only the judgment of God can be safely trusted.

## Conclusion

This psalm warns against concern over one's social status. It also warns against robbery and oppression. It reminds us that God is the sovereign Judge. He judges in terms of what we do, not where we are on society's totem pole.

# 12

# GOD IS THE SOURCE OF RAIN

*Thou visitest the earth, and waterest it: thou greatly enrichest it with the river of God, which is full of water: thou preparest them corn, when thou hast so provided for it. Thou waterest the ridges thereof abundantly: thou settlest the furrows thereof: thou makest it soft with showers: thou blessest the springing thereof. Thou crownest the year with thy goodness; and thy paths drop fatness.*

PSALM 65:9–11

When we search for the god of a particular society, we should first examine the society's concept of covenant. The five-point biblical covenant exists in an altered form in every society.

It is sometimes said that the source of law is the god of a society.[1] Law is point three of the biblical covenant.[2] It can equally be said that the source of the sanctions of the legal order is the god of a society.[3] So intertwined are society's ethical standards and its sanctions that the two should be considered as a unit. Therefore, we can say that the source of law and sanctions in a society is the god of a society. What people believe about the source of law and law's sanctions in history is important as a means of identifying what kind of god that members of a particular society believe in. The theocentric issue here is sanctions.

---

1. T. Robert Ingram, *The World Under God's Law* (Houston, Texas: St. Thomas Press, 1962), p. 3; R. J. Rushdoony, *The Institutes of Biblical Law* (Nutley, New Jersey: Craig Press, 1973), p. 4.

2. Ray R. Sutton, *That You May Prosper: Dominion By Covenant*, 2nd ed. (Tyler, Texas: Institute for Christian Economics, [1987] 1992), ch. 3. Gary North, *Unconditional Surrender: God's Program for Victory*, 5th ed. (Powder Springs, Georgia: Point Five Press, [1980] 2010), ch. 3.

3. *Ibid.*, ch. 4.

53

## A. The Source of Water

In this psalm, we learn that God visits the earth and waters it. He enriches it with what the psalmist calls the river of God. This river is full of water. God also prepares grain. God is the source of both water and food. The psalmist speaks of God as actively intervening in history to provide water. God is said to water the ridges abundantly. He makes the land soft with showers. Then the psalmist declares with finality that God is the source of the goodness of the entire year. He describes the paths of society as marked by fatness.

### 1. Water, Life, and Prosperity

The psalmist says that God is the source of water. God supplies water, which in turn sustains prosperity and ultimately sustains life. God is therefore the source of life, for God is the ultimate agent in the universe. He, not autonomous nature, is the source of life. *There is no such thing as autonomous nature.* The psalmist, by proclaiming God is the source of water, is declaring that nature has no existence apart from God.

God is the source of sanctions in society, meaning the positive sanctions of life and agricultural prosperity. As the source of the positive sanctions of life and agricultural prosperity, God is therefore the God of society. To the extent that men retain faith in this psalm, they cannot maintain faith in autonomous nature. God is the source of the blessings and society, and nature is only a secondary cause.

The psalmist also declares that God waters the pastures of the wilderness. Men do not till the fields of the wilderness. He says that the little hills rejoice on every side. Obviously, this is not to be taken literally. Hills do not rejoice. The psalmist's point is that nature is subordinate to God, dependent on God, and produces nothing apart from God. If this is true of nature, then it is true of society in general.

### 2. Water on Mars

The psalmist extols God as the direct source of water. Without water, there is no life. Humanists understand the centrality of this claim. In the final decades of the twentieth century and the first decade of the twenty-first, the United States government spent billions of dollars to fund unmanned probes to Mars. The goal of this program was never stated publicly, but almost every press release related to the Mars probes indicate what the goal was. The goal was to discover water on Mars. Constantly, the reports have said that there are indications that long in the past, there was water on Mars. The evidence is extremely thin—almost as thin as the atmosphere on Mars.[4]

There is no question what the underlying purpose of the probes is: the discovery of the basis of life. Without the water, biological scientists do not believe that there can be life. So, if there are traces of water on Mars, there is supposedly the possibility of life on Mars at some time in the distant past.[5] If there was ever life on Mars, then life on the earth is not unique. If life on the earth is not unique, then God's covenants with mankind in history that relate to the unique creation of the universe, which was the background to the creation of the earth, which is the background of the creation of Adam and Eve, are not unique. This would undermine man's faith in the covenant established by God with man. It would undermine faith in the biblical story of the transition from grace to wrath (Gen. 1–3). This in turn undermines the main story of the Bible, from Genesis 3 to Revelation 20: the transition from wrath to grace. The humanists who run the United States government are determined to use the tax money of Christians to fund probes to Mars that will be used to undermine Christianity.

This psalm is an affirmation of the sovereignty of God over all creation, including society. The entire psalm is an affirmation of God as the source of the central economic blessings in history. It is therefore an affirmation of the absolute sovereignty of God.

### B. Modern Economic Theory

Such a view of economic causation is foreign to all modern economic theory. Economists trace all productivity to two sources: land and labor.[6] The universe is assumed to be autonomous, and therefore man's world is autonomous. Man is believed to be the product of the world, and therefore man is autonomous from God. He is not autonomous from nature, nor is nature autonomous from man. The interrelationship between man and nature is an autonomous process, virtually all economic theory asserts. In any textbook in any university in any department of economics, there is no reference to God as being the

---

4. A typical example: Kenneth Chang, "Scientists Find Signs Water Is Flowing on Mars," *New York Times* (Aug. 4, 2011). On January 30, 2012, I searched Google for "Mars Probe" and "water." I got this result: about 500,000 hits.

5. "Mars Probe Confirms Water on Ancient Mars—Is Proof of Life Next?" *Daily Galaxy* (Dec. 9, 2011).

6. Murray N. Rothbard, *Man, Economy, and State: A Treatise on Economic Principles*, 2nd ed. (Auburn, Alabama: Mises Institute, [1962] 2009), ch. 5:4.

source of the productivity of both land and labor. God is considered to be a hypothesis that cannot be verified by scientific methodology. Because economists regard economics as a science, they self-consciously strip all references to God out of the curriculum.

William Letwin argued that economics was the first social science to be self-conscious in its rejection of any concept of God or morality. He argued that early economic theory was a self-conscious reaction against the English Civil War, which was fought on the basis of rival views of Christianity. Late seventeenth-century economics was an attempt to create a science of society which did not invoke either Christianity or the Bible. Economists believed that there could be no reconciliation between rival theories of Christianity and the Bible. So, they self-consciously attempted to separate economic theory from morality in the Bible.[7]

This psalm categorically denies the foundation of modern economic theory. There is no possibility of reconciling this psalm with modern economic theory. No matter how hard those few Christians who happen to be certified academic economists attempt to segregate economic theory from the Bible, this psalm makes it clear that *God alone is the source of economic productivity associated with nature*. Whatever man does is subordinate to what God does. If God withholds the rain, it does not matter what men do. There will be drought.

### Conclusion

This psalm extends its affirmation of God as the source of agricultural blessings to multiple blessings. In Psalm 68, we read: "Blessed be the Lord, who daily loadeth us with benefits, even the God of our salvation. Selah" (v. 19). In Psalm 85, we read: "Yea, the LORD shall give that which is good; and our land shall yield her increase" (v. 12). This confession was the basis of James' affirmation a millennium later: "Every good gift and every perfect gift is from above, and cometh down from the Father of lights, with whom is no variableness, neither shadow of turning" (James 1:17).[8]

This psalm undermines the operational presupposition of modern economic theory: the autonomy of nature and man. Economic theory must therefore be reconstructed in terms of a view of God

---

7. William Letwin, *The Origins of Scientific Economics* (Cambridge, Massachusetts: MIT Press, 1963).

8. Gary North, *Ethics and Dominion: An Economic Commentary on the Epistles* (Dallas, Georgia: Point Five Press, 2012), ch. 32.

which proclaims that He, and He alone, is the source of the rain. *There can be no autonomy for nature or mankind.* All economic theory, if it is to be accurate, must begin with the concept of God as the source of the productivity of land. This will require the rewriting of all texts and monographs related to nature as one of the two sources of productivity. Man is dependent on nature, and nature is dependent on God. Through the covenant, man gains control over nature. Therefore, man is dependent on God. This has to be the operating starting point of all economic theory, if economic theory is to be accurate. Modern economic theory implicitly begins with the assumption that this psalm cannot possibly be true literally. There is therefore an inescapable confrontation between humanistic economic theory and biblical economic theory.

## 13

# TRIED AS SILVER

*For thou, O God, hast proved us: thou hast tried us, as silver is tried. Thou broughtest us into the net; thou laidst affliction upon our loins. Thou hast caused men to ride over our heads; we went through fire and through water: but thou broughtest us out into a wealthy place.*

PSALM 66:10–12

### A. Affliction and Restoration

The psalmist presents the biblical procedure for extending the kingdom of God. There is a period of testing. It leads to a period of defeat. Then there is restoration. Restoration is a time for the visible blessings of God. This is in contrast to the time for the visible cursings of God. The theocentric issue here is sanctions.

The pre-exilic prophets came before Israel and Judah to warn the people of a time of corporate negative sanctions. The nation would be defeated militarily and carried into captivity. The prophets did not say that there was anything that the people could do to avoid this period of persecution. They promised Israel and Judah that there would be a time of restoration after the period of captivity. There was hope in the future, but not in the immediate future. There would be a time of sabbath rest for the land (Jer. 50:34), but first there would be a time of persecution and pain.

Isaiah used the imagery of silver smelting to describe what was coming. The nation had rebelled. "How is the faithful city become an harlot! it was full of judgment; righteousness lodged in it; but now murderers. Thy silver is become dross, thy wine mixed with water"

(Isa. 1:21–22).[1] Rebellion is the equivalent of debased silver—silver in need of purification. God promised to provide this purification. "And I will turn my hand upon thee, and purely purge away thy dross, and take away all thy tin: And I will restore thy judges as at the first, and thy counsellors as at the beginning: afterward thou shalt be called, The city of righteousness, the faithful city. Zion shall be redeemed with judgment, and her converts with righteousness" (Isa. 1:25–27). To regain purity, the nation needed smelting. It needed negative sanctions.

The prophets warned of captivity to come. This had been Moses' message six or seven centuries earlier.

> Then my anger shall be kindled against them in that day, and I will forsake them, and I will hide my face from them, and they shall be devoured, and many evils and troubles shall befall them; so that they will say in that day, Are not these evils come upon us, because our God is not among us? And I will surely hide my face in that day for all the evils which they shall have wrought, in that they are turned unto other gods. Now therefore write ye this song for you, and teach it the children of Israel: put it in their mouths, that this song may be a witness for me against the children of Israel. For when I shall have brought them into the land which I sware unto their fathers, that floweth with milk and honey; and they shall have eaten and filled themselves, and waxen fat; then will they turn unto other gods, and serve them, and provoke me, and break my covenant. And it shall come to pass, when many evils and troubles are befallen them, that this song shall testify against them as a witness; for it shall not be forgotten out of the mouths of their seed: for I know their imagination which they go about, even now, before I have brought them into the land which I sware (Deut. 31:17–21).[2]

### B. A Biblical Pattern

This pattern is found throughout the Bible. It is a consequence of the Fall of man. Prior to the Fall of man, there was to be a period of testing in the form of work. Adam was required to name the animals (Gen. 2:19–20) before he was given a wife (Gen. 2:21–22). There is performance before there is reward. There are requirements to which are attached sanctions. The sanctions, positive or negative, are consistent with the performance. God warned Adam that he would die if he ate from the forbidden tree. There was a command and a sanction.

---

1. Gary North, *Restoration and Dominion: An Economic Commentary on the Prophets* (Dallas, Georgia: Point Five Press, 2012), ch. 3.

2. Gary North, *Inheritance and Dominion: An Economic Commentary on Deuteronomy*, 2nd ed. (Dallas, Georgia: Point Five Press, [1999] 2012), ch. 76.

Once Adam fell, mankind was placed under a system of sanctions that substituted persecution and defeat for work. In the garden, Adam was required to work. He was not required to suffer. The requirement that he would suffer did not come until after the Fall, when God specifically punished Adam's body and his environment (Gen. 3:17–19).[3] From that time forward, mankind has worked under a curse.

When God substituted cursing for unimpeded labor, He made life more difficult for mankind. The psalmist reminds us of the message of Moses to the generation of the conquest. *Corporate ethical rebellion produces negative corporate sanctions.* The nation would therefore go into captivity.

The psalmist understood this Mosaic legal framework. He understood that Israel had suffered in the wilderness. The Amalekites had defeated them (Num. 14:45). He understood that the time of wandering had been a time of testing. God did not bring the people into the wilderness in order to destroy them, as they had repeatedly accused Him. He brought them into the wilderness in order to protect the exodus generation from enemies and also to strengthen the generation of the conquest. This was a successful venture. That generation did conquer Canaan.

The psalmist speaks of God's deliverance of the people into a wealthy land. This is another way of saying that the land possessed valuable resources. The Promised Land that had belonged to the Canaanites was set aside by God for the inheritance of His people. It took 40 years of wandering, plus a six-year war, for Israel to inherent this land. This was a time of testing. The psalmist dismisses the period of testing as irrelevant when compared to the blessings of inheriting the land of Canaan. The ends were worth the means.

The psalmist reminds his listeners that they should not pay much attention to the difficulties of life. These difficulties are part of the payment that is required for men to extend the kingdom of God in a cursed environment. Men should not give up hope that their efforts will be successful. They should be confident. This is an important message of this psalm.

## Conclusion

The process of dominion is one of testing. Things get difficult. God's goal is not judgment unto oblivion but judgment unto restoration.

---

3. Gary North, *Sovereignty and Dominion: An Economic Commentary on Genesis* (Dallas, Georgia: Point Five Press, [1982] 2012), ch. 12.

First, negative sanctions; then, positive sanctions. God delivers His people into the hands of the enemy. Then He delivers them out.

This pattern extends into the New Covenant. The bodily death-resurrection-ascension-enthronement of Jesus Christ is the model. It is the church's model for history, not eternity. The church does not pass from history into eternity on the basis of its cultural failure in history. There is continuity. The Book of Psalms, more than any other book in the Bible, affirms the historical basis of this continuity.

# 14

## SILVER AND SUBMISSION

*Because of thy temple at Jerusalem shall kings bring presents unto thee. Rebuke the company of spearmen, the multitude of the bulls, with the calves of the people, till every one submit himself with pieces of silver: scatter thou the people that delight in war.*

PSALM 68:29–30

### A. Symbols: Temple, Jerusalem, and Kings

There was never a time in which the kings of the earth came to Jerusalem to bring presents to God, which were presented at, or on behalf of, the temple. The original temple was destroyed by the invading Babylonians early in the sixth century B.C., and the rebuilt temple was destroyed by the invading Romans in 70 A.D. With the exception of a few dispensationalists, Christian expositors have argued that there is no building that serves the same purposes as the temple. So, Old Testament prophecies regarding the temple are fulfilled by the church international. These prophecies have nothing to do with Palestine. With respect to this prophecy, why will kings, whose Old Covenant office no longer exists, bring presents to Jerusalem? There is no temple today.

Jerusalem remains a city. It is not a city where kings will come to offer sacrifices. The theocentric issue here is hierarchy, yet also sacrifice.

There are also no kings. King Farouk, the puppet king of Egypt who was installed by the British in the mid-1930s, once commented, "There are only five kings in the world: the king of England, and the kings of clubs, diamonds, spades, and hearts." The last of the European kings departed immediately after World War I. The Czar of Russia was removed from office by the Bolsheviks in 1917. Royalty is no longer a factor in world affairs, except for occasional celebrations. Kings and queens today are at most minor celebrities, except in Great Britain.

With the exception of a variety of dispensationalism which teaches that there will be a reconstructed temple in the era of Jesus' millennial reign on earth, every Christian principle of interpretation (hermeneutic) insists that this passage has to be interpreted in a symbolic way. The debate is over the correct symbols.

### B. The Great Reversal

The psalmist calls on God to rebuke the company of spearmen and the multitude of the bulls. He calls on God to do this by means of the calves of the people. This is poetic language. The "company of spearmen" refers to an army. These are people who do battle for a civil government or for a warlord. The phrase, "the multitude of the bulls," could refer to invading kings. These bulls command the army of spearmen. The psalmist specifically says that he wants God to use "the calves of the people" to overcome the invading military forces. Who are they? Powerless Israelites who suffer invasion. He wants the weak to overcome the strong. Why should he want this? Because it is a testimony to the sovereignty of God whenever David defeats Goliath.

How long should the victory of the little people persist? The psalmist says that it will persist, or should persist, until everyone submits himself with pieces of silver. Who is "everyone"? The invading kings. This refers to a payment to the authorities of Israel. The payment of silver would be a token of subordination by those whom God had conquered.

When the psalmist speaks of everyone, he is referring to the company of spearmen and the multitude of the bulls. He is referring, in other words, to pagan invaders who will seek to conquer the nation of Israel. They will believe that the power of the sword is so great that they can conquer God's holy people. The psalmist rejects this outlook. He wants God to use the *common people*, whom he refers to as the *calves of the people*, to overturn publicly the spearmen and the bulls. He wants the powerful to submit to the weak, who represent God.

This theme is found throughout the Bible. I call it the great reversal. The reason why the great reversal is the preferred means of

*Great Reversal — the powerful submit to the weak.*

*So God gets all the credit.*

deliverance for the psalmist is because he wants God to get all of the credit. He wants the defeat of a strong invader to be so great that no one could cogently attribute this victory to any other force in history besides the God of the Bible.

## C. Submission

To present silver to a conqueror is an act of submission. A conqueror here submits to little people, who act on behalf of the God of the temple. This is a public manifestation of the defeated conqueror's admission that God had conquered him. This is what the psalmist wants to see.

Whenever something valuable, such as silver, is handed over to a conqueror, the person handing over the asset is publicly acknowledging his own defeat at the hands of a victor. The psalmist wants a public manifestation of the kings' representative submission to God. He wants this to take place in full public view.

## D. Anti-War

The spearmen and the secular powers behind them are warriors. The psalmist wants to see them scattered. He says specifically that he wants God to scatter the people who delight in war. This is an emphatic statement that *war is to be avoided whenever possible*. God does not delight in war. Elsewhere, we read that David was not allowed to build the temple, because he was a man of blood. He liked warfare. Such a man was not fit for building the temple of God.

> Then David the king stood up upon his feet, and said, Hear me, my brethren, and my people: As for me, I had in mine heart to build an house of rest for the ark of the covenant of the LORD, and for the footstool of our God, and had made ready for the building: But God said unto me, Thou shalt not build an house for my name, because thou hast been a man of war, and hast shed blood (I Chron. 28:2–3).

We must not say that offensive warfare in every instance is illegitimate. The conquest of Canaan was by military action. But Israel was not again called on by God to extend its borders by an act of war.

In this passage, the psalmist says that he wants people scattered who delight in war. He does not want to see them extend their influence. He wants the weak to defeat the mighty. This need not mean that the scattering process has to be military. It is quite possible that the scattering can be economic, or it can be caused by plague. The main thing the psalmist is concerned with is the message that *a nation that relies on military power to extend its kingdom is violating a fundamental biblical principle.* The psalmist calls for the overthrow of warmongers.

This passage extols *nonviolence*. The psalmist is hostile to people who delight in war. So is God. While war is sometimes necessary to defend a particular territory, the use of military violence to extend the kingdom of God was limited under the Old Covenant, and it is never recommended in the New Covenant. The covenant of Jesus Christ is a covenant based on hearing. Paul tells us that faith comes by hearing, and hearing by the word of God (Rom. 10:17). Preaching and discipling are to be Christendom's tools of dominion. Men are to preach the gospel of deliverance from sin and discipline their subordinates in terms of the principles of biblical law.

The psalmist is saying that the power of God is sufficient to scatter violent invaders. God honors the nation of Israel by raising up common people to expel the invaders. War is not to become a means for extending the kingdom of God in history.

### Conclusion

The rulers of the nations will someday confess their subordination to the God of the Bible. They will do so by presenting their tithes to the church. This will be in history, when sin still exists and civil governments that restrict it still exist. It therefore cannot refer to the world beyond the grave.

Amillennialists interpret this passage as referring to the final judgment. The difficulty with this passage from an amillennial standpoint is this: during the era of the final judgment, there will be no kings. Kings were an aspect of civil government under the Old Covenant. Civil government deals with the suppression of covenant-breaking acts. There will be no covenant-breaking acts during or after the final judgment. The next verse refers to people who delight in war. There will be no war at the final judgment, although there may be one just before. This passage is one of the most difficult of all passages in the Bible for the amillennialist.

# 15

## DELIVERANCE FROM POVERTY

*But I am poor and needy: make haste unto me, O God: thou art my help and my deliverer; O LORD, make no tarrying.* 7/25/2023

PSALM 70:5

### A. Avoiding Poverty

The theocentric issue here is sanctions. Sanctions are the basis of inheritance or disinheritance. This passage makes it clear that poverty is something to be avoided. *Poverty is a restriction on a person's ability to extend the kingdom of God in history*. It also makes it difficult to enjoy the blessings that God promises to His covenant people. Poverty is not something to be attained through some form of spiritual exercise. The correct goal for a covenant-keeping person is not to master the condition of poverty; it is to master the techniques for escaping poverty legally.

In Proverbs, we read a prayer against poverty.

> Two things have I required of thee; deny me them not before I die: Remove far from me vanity and lies: give me neither poverty nor riches; feed me with food convenient for me: Lest I be full, and deny thee, and say, Who is the LORD? or lest I be poor, and steal, and take the name of my God in vain (Prov. 30:7–9).[1]

The author fears that if he is reduced to a condition of poverty, he may be tempted to steal. On the other hand, the same passage dismisses the quest for riches. The author fears that if he attains great

---

1. Gary North, Wisdom *and Dominion: An Economic Commentary on Proverbs* (Dallas, Georgia: Point Five Press, [2007] 2012), ch. 84.

66

riches, he will be tempted to forget God. So, on the one hand, poverty is a good motivation for overcoming poverty. It is a condition to be overcome. On the other hand, the goal of the overcomer should not be the amassing of great wealth. The goal of poverty is to escape poverty by means of God's grace and by means of those principles of covenant-keeping discipleship that produce wealth. The goal is not to produce wealth for its own sake, but rather to enable the victim of poverty to escape, and then give God the credit for the escape.

## B. God's Covenantal Authority

This passage explicitly calls on God to deliver the poor person from his condition of poverty. The psalmist declares that God has the power to do this, so it would be foolish for a poor person not to call upon God to deliver him from a condition that is associated with Adam's curse. It is a curse when God removes the tools of dominion from a covenant-keeping person. One of the tools of dominion is capital. If a person cannot afford capital, he is restricted in his use of physical and conceptual tools of dominion.

The primary tools of deliverance out of poverty are not purchased in an open market. They include confidence regarding the future by means of the sovereignty of God and biblical law. There is also confidence that God brings positive sanctions to those who conform themselves to the standards of biblical law. These are matters of verbal confession and internal faith, not matters of competitive bidding in an open market. *These are matters of faith, not matters of commerce.* At the same time, these matters of faith can, do, and should affect the world of commerce.

Deuteronomy 28:1–14 assures us that covenant-keeping produces blessings in history. One of these blessings is increased wealth. "The LORD shall open unto thee his good treasure, the heaven to give the rain unto thy land in his season, and to bless all the work of thine hand: and thou shalt lend unto many nations, and thou shalt not borrow" (v. 12). Deuteronomy 28:15–68 stands in contrast to the first section. This section lists the curses of God, and among these curses is poverty.

> Thine ox shall be slain before thine eyes, and thou shalt not eat thereof: thine ass shall be violently taken away from before thy face, and shall not be restored to thee: thy sheep shall be given unto thine enemies, and thou shalt have none to rescue them (v. 31).

CONFIDENCE AND DOMIONION: PSALMS

> Thou shalt plant vineyards, and dress them, but shalt neither drink of the wine, nor gather the grapes; for the worms shall eat them (v. 39).

> All thy trees and fruit of thy land shall the locust consume (v. 42).

For a covenant-keeper to find himself in a condition of poverty is to find a reason to call upon God to deliver him. *Poverty becomes a test of a covenant-keeper's commitment to the covenant.* The covenant declares that a sovereign God rules the universe, and He governs the universe in terms of biblical law. When we call on God to deliver us from poverty, we implicitly call upon God to uphold His law. We call on Him to impose positive sanctions on acts of covenant-keeping. It is a call based on confidence that the universe is not impersonal, that it operates in terms of the biblical covenant, and that God, as absolutely sovereign, is capable of eradicating poverty in the life of anyone who conforms himself to the stipulations of the covenant.

The psalmist is declaring his faith that God does intervene in history to deliver His people from the curse of poverty. This is not a program of "think and grow rich." On the contrary, it is a program that denies the legitimacy of thinking to grow rich. This program relies on a concept of a sovereign God who intervenes in history on behalf of His people. The psalmist finds himself in dire straits. He does not curse the dire straits; he praises God and calls upon God to deliver him from dire straits. He sees dire straits as an opportunity to call upon the God of the covenant to uphold the terms of His covenant and deliver him from the burden of poverty.

The passage calls upon God to intervene directly. This is not a call for national repentance. It is not a call for revolution. It is not a call for political action. It is simply a call for God to intervene and deliver the psalmist from the affliction of poverty. This is not pie in the sky by and by. This is an affirmation of the sovereignty of God. It is an affirmation that says that God is capable of intervening into the affairs of men to deliver covenant-keepers from the affliction of poverty.

## C. Humanist Economics

Here we see a profound difference between biblical economics and humanist economics. Humanist economists call on men, not on God. Humanist economists see poverty as something to be avoided. They see it as something that should be overcome in history. They believe that specific programs will enable the bulk of people who are trapped in poverty to escape poverty over time. They do not call on God to deliver an individual poor person from dire straits. They believe that there are predictable patterns of behavior and specific social and political arrangements that will, over time, enable the vast majority of individuals to escape from poverty. So, they do not call upon God to intervene directly into the lives of the poor. They may call upon the state to intervene in specific areas, such as the enforcement of contracts, so that the innate creativity of individuals should be allowed to flourish.

Their goal is to reform individuals through the reform of civil institutions. Economists offer specific and competing programs of reform that are said to reduce the level of poverty per capita wherever these reforms are implemented. The Bible does not speak about such reforms. It speaks about the defense of property by means of laws against theft and violence. But the Bible does not make widespread deliverance from poverty one of its primary themes. The modern world does. The modern world therefore stands in contrast to the Bible's call for divine intervention. It calls for individuals to conform themselves to the standards of the marketplace or, in the case of socialism, to the standards of the central planners.

*Humanist economics is impersonal economics.* It does not affirm a sovereign God who has established specific laws and who threatens to impose specific negative sanctions for violations of these laws. Humanism's sovereign agent is man, either individual man in the case of free market economists, or else collective man in the case of socialist economists. In both cases, man is sovereign; God is not only not sovereign, He is rarely mentioned. He is analytically useless. He is to be dismissed by means of Occam's razor. He is not necessary to the hypothesis. He is extra baggage.

The psalmist says that God is the deliverer. This includes deliverance from poverty. He calls upon God to intervene in history to deliver him from the burden of poverty. This is a legitimate prayer. An individual wants to be delivered from poverty for multiple reasons, but the biblical reason, according to Jesus, is to seek first the kingdom of God and His righteousness. All the other things, meaning the trappings of wealth, will be added by God in response to covenant-keeping and prayer (Matt 6:33).[2]

The goal is not "more for me in history." That is the confession of Mammon, not the confession of God. Man's goal should be to escape

---

2. Gary North, *Priorities and Dominion: An Economic Commentary on Matthew*, 2nd ed. (Dallas, Georgia: Point Five Pres, [2000] 2012), ch. 15.

poverty for the sake of God's kingdom, not man's kingdom. His goal should also be to escape riches, for exactly the same reason. Biblical economics is theocentric, not anthropocentric. The universe revolves around God, not around man. He who forgets this risks poverty.

### Conclusion

A covenant-keeper should have confidence that poverty can be overcome. The conquest of poverty begins with an affirmation of the covenant. Specifically, it begins with a prayer to God for deliverance. It does not begin with a program of corporate reform—social, economic, or political.

"Deliver me, O Lord, from poverty."

7/25/2023

# 16

## GODLY RULE

*He shall judge thy people with righteousness, and thy poor with judgment. The mountains shall bring peace to the people, and the little hills, by righteousness. He shall judge the poor of the people, he shall save the children of the needy, and shall break in pieces the oppressor.*

PSALM 72:2-4

The theocentric issue here is God as the judge. Psalm 72 is a messianic psalm. It begins with a description of the messianic ruler. This ruler exercises civil authority. He is not a priest. Or, if he is a priest, he is a priest who bears civil authority. The priesthood under the Mosaic law was associated with the tribe of Levi. The civil magistrate was associated with the tribe of Judah. Jacob prophesied: "The sceptre shall not depart from Judah, nor a lawgiver from between his feet, until Shiloh come; and unto him shall the gathering of the people be" (Gen. 49:10). Under the Mosaic law, the two offices were separate. In the New Covenant, the two offices belong to Jesus Christ. He is the fulfillment of Jacob's prophecy. He is the Messiah; therefore, He is the head of both church and state.

### A. Protector of the Poor

The ruler described in this passage is a righteous man. The psalmist specifically identifies the poor as the beneficiaries of his rulership. "He shall judge the poor of the people, he shall save the children of the needy, and shall break in pieces the oppressor" (v. 4). This is powerful language. Here is a judge who smashes to pieces all oppressors. Obviously, this is not to be taken literally. The messianic ruler does not put all oppressors into a deep freeze storage unit, and then use a hammer to smash them in pieces. The imagery is that of conquest. Another example of it in the Mosaic law is the term "rod of iron." The rod of iron breaks to pieces all those who break covenant with the God of the Bible.

This may sound like a program of political reform. The passage could be used to promote state intervention to confiscate the wealth of anyone, merely because he is wealthy, to give to the poor. This interpretation does not do justice to the passage. The evil person described here is not said to be rich; he is said to be an oppressor. An oppressor, biblically speaking, is a person who misuses the civil government in order to achieve his own ends. He uses violence or the threat of violence by the government in order to benefit himself.[1] This is the mark of injustice. The individual described in this passage is a just ruler, and so he will smash oppressors.

One of the benefits of living under the rule of the Messiah will be peace. This is a condition of permanent peace. It will last as long as the moon endures (v. 5). This is a mark of a peaceful kingdom. It has never come to this earth so far. This is clearly a messianic psalm. It applies to some future era of kingdom righteousness.

Verse eight says that he shall have dominion. He will rule from sea to sea and from the river to the end of the earth. This is an affirmation of his universal dominion. This is dominion that expands across all of humanity. This is not a ruler who operates in one nation or one tribe. This ruler is king over all the earth. He exercises dominion across the whole face of the earth.[2]

The psalmist says that his enemies will *lick the dust*. This is a symbolic reference to their *complete subordination*. The language applies to a condition of universal justice and universal peace. This is not necessarily a one-world civil government, but it is clearly a *one-world kingdom*. It is government in the sense of jurisdiction from on high. The premillennialist argues that Jesus Christ will reappear bodily and exercise such judgment over an international bureaucratic system of law. The postmillennialist argues that this judgment comes through Christ's earthly representatives, in time and on earth. It is representative rule, not direct rule. The amillennialist says that God's judgment of covenant-breakers comes only at the end of time.

1. Gary North, *Authority and Dominion: An Economic Commentary on Exodus* (Dallas, Georgia: Point Five Press, 2012), Part 3, *Tools of Dominion* (1990), ch. 48.

2. Kenneth Gentry, *He Shall Have Dominion: A Postmillennial Eschatology*, 2nd ed.(Tyler, Texas: Institute for Christian Economics, [1992] 1997).

The other kings will bring him presents. This indicates universal dominion. There are other civil governments operating, but they are under the jurisdiction of the Messiah. The kings of the earth show that they are subordinate to the Messiah because they bring tokens of this subordination: presents. This is a form of political tribute, but it is a symbolic token of subordination. The amillennialist spiritualizes the passage, i.e., denies that it will ever come true in history.

The psalmist once again invokes the plight of the needy. This ruler will deliver the needy when the needy cry out for justice. The same is true of the poor, to the extent that a poor man economically is different from a needy person, whose need may be different from a lack of money. He delivers the poor person who has no helper. This indicates that the mark of a rich man is his employment of servants. This ruler will spare the poor and the needy. This means that he will deliver them from evildoers, men who had previously occupied positions of civil authority. He will redeem the souls of the poor from deceit and violence. This does not mean spiritual redemption. A civil ruler is not in a position to grant salvation as part of his office. He is in a position to protect them from deceit and violence; this is the mark of civil authority.

He will receive the gold of Sheba (v. 10). This was fulfilled specifically by Solomon (I Kings 10:10). Sheba is no more. Solomon was a righteous judge, but he did not rule across the face of the earth. He did not rule from sea to sea. What he did was representative of what the messianic ruler will do when he exercises universal authority.

This was the final prayer of David the son of Jesse (v. 20). He had been a king, so he knew the responsibilities of exercising civil authority. He knew the pitfalls. He was asserting his confidence that there will be a king greater than he in the future.

## Conclusion

Godly rule involves enforcing biblical law on all violators. The poor, when victims, are entitled to justice in the courts. A godly ruler will impose God's laws without consideration of the wealth of the citizens. The courts will be predictable. This is the rule of law.[3]

---

3. North, *Authority and Dominion*, ch. 50.

## 17

## THE SLIPPERY SLOPE

*For I was envious at the foolish, when I saw the prosperity of the wicked. For there are no bands in their death: but their strength is firm. They are not in trouble as other men; neither are they plagued like other men.*

PSALM 73:2–4

### A. Why Evil Men Prosper

Psalm 73 speaks to the issue of why evil men prosper. Leviticus 26 and Deuteronomy 28 present a different picture. They begin with a relatively short list of blessings that come to covenant-keepers. Both spend most of the chapter dealing with curses that come to covenant-breakers. What bothers the psalmist here is that covenant-breakers seem to prosper, while covenant-keepers do not.

The importance of this psalm is that it returns at the end to the framework described in Leviticus 26 and Deuteronomy 28. The psalmist concludes that he had been foolish for paying attention to the success of covenant-breakers. He says that their success is in fact a trap set by God to ensnare them. He uses the phrase "slippery places" (v. 18). He sees the prosperity of the wicked as a trap established by God in order to confirm His covenant.

The psalmist says that foolish and wicked people do not experience trouble as other men do (v. 5). They are not plagued with the same sorts of crises. He is speaking here about rich people. But most people in history are not rich. In every society ever studied, a relatively small percentage of the population owns most of the capital goods. This is called the Pareto 20/80 rule. It was discovered by sociologist-economist Vilfredo Pareto in the late nineteenth century. He

74

published his findings in 1897. There have been no exceptions to his description of the distribution of capital in every Western, industrial society.

The majority of foolish and wicked people remain poor. They do not get rich. The ones who do get rich become the focus of concern for people who are distressed by the fact that covenant-breaking seems to prosper. Covenant-keepers want to believe that our world is governed by a sovereign God who rewards covenant-keeping and punishes covenant-breaking. This is taught explicitly in Leviticus 26 and Deuteronomy 28.

The psalmist says in verse 12 that the ungodly prosper in this world. They increase in riches. In verse 13, he says that he cleanses his heart in vain. He has washed his hands in innocency. In verse 14, he says that he has been plagued and chastened every morning. In verse 16, he says that the knowledge of this was painful to him. This led him into the sanctuary of God, and there he understood the end of covenant-breakers (v. 17).

In the language of the King James Version, God has set these people in slippery places. He casts them down into destruction (v. 18). God actively intervenes to destroy them. Ours is not a universe governed by cosmic impersonalism. It is a universe governed by a sovereign God who upholds His law by bringing sanctions against those who break it. In verse 19, the psalmist says that these people are brought to desolation in a moment. They become consumed with terror. The picture here is of a person who is flying high and then crashes. There is almost no interval between the high flying and the crashing.

### B. Out of Darkness

In verse 21, he says that his heart had been grieved. The reason his heart had been grieved was that he was foolish. He admits this in verse 22. He says that he was as a beast before God. In other words, he was completely ignorant. He did not understand the full operations of covenantal cause and effect. He implies that he was deceived by the same deception with which God deceives the covenant-breakers.

The psalmist was upset initially because he accepted the description of ethical cause and effect that Moses presented in Leviticus 26 and Deuteronomy 28. He did not understand that God actively intervenes in history to deceive covenant-breakers. God is willing to allow them to prosper for season, only to bring them down without warning in a moment. Their productivity and their success keep them from acknowledging that their blessings come only from the hand of God. God takes this arrogance and uses it against them. They make a mistake. They do not see a disaster coming. They are blind to what is about to overtake them, because they are blind to the ethical cause-and-effect nature of human affairs.

The psalmist is warning covenant-keepers not to make the same mistake that covenant-breakers are deliberately led to believe by God. It is not that God merely allows them to make these mistakes. The psalmist says, "Surely thou didst set them in slippery places." This is a *deliberate policy* of God to keep people from understanding the truth of their own situation. It is deliberate on God's part that these people not see that they have been placed in slippery places.

The psalmist then praises God. He says that God has held him by his right hand. He affirms that God will guide him with counsel and afterward receive him to glory. In other words, he affirms what Moses declares in the early sections of Leviticus 26 and Deuteronomy 28. What had confused him for a time no longer confuses him. It seemed as though the covenantal cause-and-effect structure of human affairs was being violated by the success of covenant-breakers. No longer is the psalmist confused. He sees now that it is all a part of God's plan. God specifically sets up covenant-breakers in positions of authority and wealth, only to tear them down later.

God does tell people about the nature of His cause-and-effect system of governing. But when people suppress the truth in unrighteousness, which the apostle Paul says that they do (Rom. 1:18), this suppression leads to their destruction. God sees that these people will not accept the truth, and so He uses positive sanctions in order to lower them into decisions that will produce negative sanctions. He raises them up in order to tear them down.

Few Christians view God in this way. They view Him as laying down the law and then standing aside to see what people will do. The psalmist asserts the opposite. He says that God sets people up— people who do not deserve to be raised to positions of wealth and influence. God does this deliberately to trick them, so that they will not see the disaster that is heading for them.

Isaiah said the same thing about presenting the prophetic message to the Israelites.

> Also I heard the voice of the Lord, saying, Whom shall I send, and who will go for us? Then said I, Here am I; send me. And he said, Go, and tell this people, Hear ye indeed, but understand not; and see ye indeed, but

perceive not. Make the heart of this people fat, and make their ears heavy, and shut their eyes; lest they see with their eyes, and hear with their ears, and understand with their heart, and convert, and be healed (Isa. 6:8–10).

Jesus quoted this in Matthew 13 in answer to the question from the apostles about why He spoke in parables. He told them that He spoke in parables so that the Israelites would not understand what He was saying and therefore repent.

Therefore speak I to them in parables: because they seeing see not; and hearing they hear not, neither do they understand. And in them is fulfilled the prophecy of Esaias, which saith, By hearing ye shall hear, and shall not understand; and seeing ye shall see, and shall not perceive: For this people's heart is waxed gross, and their ears are dull of hearing, and their eyes they have closed; lest at any time they should see with their eyes, and hear with their ears, and should understand with their heart, and should be converted, and I should heal them. But blessed are your eyes, for they see: and your ears, for they hear (Matt. 13:13–16).

The Apostle Paul cited Isaiah when he spoke to the Jews for the last time, at the end of the Book of Acts. Some believed his message; some did not.

And when they agreed not among themselves, they departed, after that Paul had spoken one word, Well spake the Holy Ghost by Esaias the prophet unto our fathers, Saying, Go unto this people, and say, Hearing ye shall hear, and shall not understand; and seeing ye shall see, and not perceive: For the heart of this people is waxed gross, and their ears are dull of hearing, and their eyes have they closed; lest they should see with their eyes, and hear with their ears, and understand with their heart, and should be converted, and I should heal them. Be it known therefore unto you, that the salvation of God is sent unto the Gentiles, and that they will hear it. And when he had said these words, the Jews departed, and had great reasoning among themselves (Acts 28:25–29).

Again, this is not how most people, especially Christians, view the way that God deals with covenant-breakers. Yet it is how God has said He deals with them. It is how the psalmist said God deals with them. I think a wise conclusion is that this is the way He deals with them.

This is why we should not be concerned by the fact that covenant-breakers prosper more than covenant-keepers. The success of covenant-breakers is not only temporary, it is a trap. The positive sanctions that they receive from God are in fact *disguised negative sanctions.* These accumulate over time, and they produce failure.

We can therefore have confidence that the world is governed by a system of ethical cause and effect. This is not an impersonal system of causation; it is a system actively governed by God. So actively is it governed by God, that God sometimes allows what appears to be a violation of His system of ethical cause and effect. Yet, in the end, it is not a violation of the system; it is an affirmation of the system.

## Conclusion

Leviticus 26 and Deuteronomy 28 were the background for the psalmist's concern over the economic success of the wicked. He learned in the sanctuary that God had not abandoned the covenantal system described in Leviticus 26 and Deuteronomy 28. Not only does God still enforce it, He uses it against covenant-breakers. He sets them up by abandoning this structure of causation for a time, only to spring the covenantal trap on them without warning. Causation is not ethically random. It is not covenantally random. It is covenantally structured. He who argues otherwise must reject this psalm, either as it applied in the Old Covenant or in the New Covenant. He must reject its relevance in the New Covenant era. I ask: On what basis? I also ask: Are all the psalms equally irrelevant in terms of historical causation? If not, why not? I suggest that you also ask anyone who rejects this psalm's conclusions regarding historical causation. See if the answer is better than this: "Because I just don't like the idea of historical causation being both providential and covenantal. That would make me responsible for lots of things that I prefer to ignore. I don't want any extra responsibilities. I would prefer even fewer."

# 18

## PROTECTING THE WEAK

*Have respect unto the covenant: for the dark places of the earth are full of the habitations of cruelty. O let not the oppressed return ashamed: let the poor and needy praise thy name.*

PSALM 74:20−21

### A. A Call for Sanctions

The theocentric issue here is God as a judge. Psalm 74 is in the form of a lamentation. The psalmist declares that evildoers have been oppressing the entire society. They have gotten into power, and they are ruthless in tearing down all traces of God's covenant. They have broken up the carved work of skilled craftsmen (v. 6). They have cast fire into the sanctuary (v. 7), presumably meaning that they have burned down local synagogues (v. 8). They have defiled sanctuaries and synagogues wherever the name of God was being honored. They are systematic in this. They work together to burn down all traces of worship.

At the same time, God has removed all prophets from the land. No one is present who can forecast how long these evil actions will go on.

The psalmist asks God how long the adversaries of God will be able to reproach God (v. 10). Shall the enemy blaspheme God's name forever (v. 10)? It is clear the psalmist does not believe this is possible. These are rhetorical questions that are designed to persuade God to take action to defend His name.

The psalmist is concerned that God's sanctions are being withheld. The evildoers are getting more powerful, and righteous people are being ever-more oppressed. So, he asks God rhetorically: "Why withdrawest thou thy hand, even thy right hand? pluck it out of thy bosom" (v. 11). He declares that God is his king of old, who works salvation in the midst of the earth (v. 12).

He then describes God's deliverances in the past. God divided the sea by His strength (v. 13). This refers to the parting of the Red Sea. He says that He broke the heads of dragons in the waters. In other words, God is all-powerful. He controls nature. He controls the flood and the rain (v. 15). Everything belongs to God, night and day (v. 16).

Foolish people have blasphemed God's name, he reminds God. The enemy has reproached God (v. 18). By recounting these sins, the psalmist expects to persuade God to take action on His own behalf.

## B. Invoking the Poor

He then invokes the poor. He speaks of the congregation of the poor. Then he reminds God to have respect for His covenant. Why? Because "the dark places of the earth are full of the habitations of cruelty" (20). This means that evil deeds are being practiced on a widespread basis.

Then he calls on God not to let the oppressed return ashamed. He says to let the poor and needy praise God's name (v. 21). Why should the poor and needy praise God's name? Because of the intervention of God in history on their behalf. Again, the psalmist is attempting to persuade God to enter the affairs of men and impose the sanctions of His covenant on evildoers. The psalm has no relevance if there is no covenant or if the covenant does not promise that God will impose positive sanctions on covenant-keepers and negative sanctions on covenant-breakers. *If the covenant has no historical sanctions, the arguments used by the psalmist are irrelevant.*

He calls on God to arise and plead His own cause (v. 22). This is an appeal to the sovereignty of God: point one of the biblical covenant.[1] Foolish people are reproaching Him every day. This should be sufficient cause for God to enforce the terms of His covenant.

The psalm ends with a request: "Forget not the voice of mine enemies: the tumult of those that rise up against the increase is continually" (v. 23). There seems to be nothing that can stop these people from continually challenging God. The only thing that can stop them

---

1. Ray R. Sutton, *That You May Prosper: Dominion By Covenant*, 2nd ed. (Tyler, Texas: Institute for Christian Economics, [1987] 1992), ch. 1. Gary North, *Unconditional Surrender: God's Program for Victory*, 5th ed. (Powder Springs, Georgia: American Vision, [1980] 2010), ch. 1.

is God. The psalmist therefore uses rhetoric and logic to persuade God to invoke the sanctions that His covenant promises.

Then the psalmist invokes the poor and the needy. He believes that God will defend the poor and the needy. God has respect for the weak people in His covenants. The covenants are filled with people of all income levels and wealth. The psalmist knows that God is especially concerned about the welfare of the poor and the needy. God recognizes that they are defenseless. They are easily oppressed. The psalmist reminds God that oppression is going on, and that in order to defend the poor and the needy, God will have to intervene into the affairs of men.

## Conclusion

This psalm places the oppressed, the poor, and the needy at the forefront. The psalmist believes that God is especially concerned about these defenseless people. By appealing to God's sense of justice to act on their behalf, the psalmist seeks to reverse the power of oppressors, blasphemers, and scoffers.

# 19

# MIRACLES AND DISCONTENTMENT

*He brought streams also out of the rock, and caused waters to run down like rivers. And they sinned yet more against him by provoking the most High in the wilderness. And they tempted God in their heart by asking meat for their lust. Yea, they spake against God; they said, Can God furnish a table in the wilderness? Behold, he smote the rock, that the waters gushed out, and the streams overflowed; can he give bread also? can he provide flesh for his people?*

PSALM 78:16–20

The theocentric issue here is God as the sanctions-bringer. The psalmist's account of the manna in the wilderness provides a good summary of events that seem difficult to explain. Liberal theologians have difficulties explaining the existence of the manna. What the psalmist refers to as angels' food (v. 25), at least one liberal theologian has described as insect excrement of two species: one in the mountains and the other in the lowlands.[1] This surely is a major difference of interpretation.

## A. Ungrateful Israel

What seems difficult to believe in retrospect is the lack of gratitude on the part of the Israelites. Moses told the generation of the inheritance that they and their parents had wandered through the wilderness by means of a series of miracles. Their feet did not swell. Their clothing did not wear out. They were given manna to eat (Deut. 8:3–4). Yet, during the early phase of the wandering, Israel complained about the lack of meat.

---

1. F. S. Bodenheimer, "The Manna of Sinai," *The Biblical Archeologist*, X (Feb. 1947); reprinted in G. Ernest Wright and David Noel Freedman (eds.), *The Biblical Archeological Reader* (Garden City, New York: Doubleday Anchor, 1961), pp. 76–79.

> And the mixt multitude that was among them fell a lusting: and the children of Israel also wept again, and said, Who shall give us flesh to eat? We remember the fish, which we did eat in Egypt freely; the cucumbers, and the melons, and the leeks, and the onions, and the garlick: But now our soul is dried away: there is nothing at all, beside this manna, before our eyes (Num. 11:4–6).

The Israelites had highly selective memories regarding their life in Egypt. They had been slaves. These complaints indicated that life was really rather good in Egypt by comparison. Forgotten were their pleas to God to be delivered (Ex. 3:7–8).

> And the LORD said, I have surely seen the affliction of my people which are in Egypt, and have heard their cry by reason of their taskmasters; for I know their sorrows; And I am come down to deliver them out of the hand of the Egyptians, and to bring them up out of that land unto a good land and a large, unto a land flowing with milk and honey; unto the place of the Canaanites, and the Hittites, and the Amorites, and the Perizzites, and the Hivites, and the Jebusites (Ex. 3:7–8).

God gave them meat: the flesh of birds. They ate to their fill. "And while the flesh was yet between their teeth, ere it was chewed, the wrath of the LORD was kindled against the people, and the LORD smote the people with a very great plague" (Num. 11:33). God set them up. Then He tore them down.

### B. Discontented Israel

In this passage, the psalmist describes their mental attitude. They were not content with water from a rock. They asked whether or not God could provide bread by means of the manna. God provided bread. The people then asked rhetorically, "Can He provide flesh for His people?" Whatever God provided by means of an astounding miracle, the Israelites dismissed as barely worth talking about. They wanted more. They were not going to be content with less. "Therefore the Lord heard this, and was wroth: so a fire was kindled against Jacob, and anger also came against Israel" (v. 21).

### 1. Unbelief

Why was God so angry with them? "Because they believed not in God, and trusted not in his salvation" (v. 22). But who did they imagine had performed miracles of deliverance and miracles of maintenance? They had already revealed what they believed in: the gods represented by the golden calf.

They saw that a series of miracles were sustaining them. Nevertheless, they judged God as being tight-fisted, because they could not
get all of what they wanted exactly when they wanted it. They were
dissatisfied with whatever it was that God had provided.

This outlook is common to mankind in most societies. Men grow
accustomed to whatever it is that they possess, and they are discontented about all that they do not possess. They are not satisfied with
what they own; they are dissatisfied because of what they do not own.
Man becomes accustomed to whatever he possesses, and he seeks
even more. Man cannot be satiated. His wants are unbounded.

## 2. Economic Theory

The fact that a man's wants are infinite is one of the foundational
principles of free market economics. This infinitude of wants is compared with the finitude of supply. At zero price, there is greater demand than supply. This is a fundamental law of economics. *The discrepancy between men's wants and their possessions is at the heart of the
economists' concept of scarcity.*

God understood that this attitude of the Israelites pointed to rebellion against Him. They tempted Him verbally, implying that He
was incapable of producing that which they did not yet possess. They
rated God's performance, not by His miracles and the plenitude of
what they possessed in a barren wilderness, but rather by what they
did not yet possess. They did not see God as being great in providing them with abundance in the midst of a barren wilderness. They
saw God as being half a god because He had not yet provided them
with more than they remembered as having possessed in Egypt. They
looked back to Egypt, and they invented a mental picture of a world
of abundance which, as slaves, they had not enjoyed. This also made
them discontented.

It was not just that the Israelites were insatiable. It was the fact
that they dismissed God's provisioning of them as evidence of a god
who is less than omnipotent. The Israelites were trapped by the religion of Mammon (Matt. 6:24–25).[2] The confession of faith of a dedicated Mammonite is this: *more for me in history.* Despite the fact that
they were wandering in the wilderness, the Israelites were convinced
that God owed them far more than He had provided. They looked at
the manna, they tasted the manna, and they concluded that it was just

---

2. Gary North, *Priorities and Dominion: An Economic Commentary on Matthew,* 2nd ed.
(Dallas, Georgia: Point Five Press, [2000] 2012), ch. 14.

too plain to meet their standards. "But now our soul is dried away: there is nothing at all, beside this manna, before our eyes" (Num. 11:6). They wanted meat. God gave them meat, in the form of birds. Then He brought a plague on them (Num. 11:33).

The religion of Mammon produces discontented people. This discontentment can be a powerful motivating force in the quest for greater wealth. This, in turn, leads to entrepreneurship. The way to profit in a free market economy is to provide goods and services to people who have the right to search elsewhere. Ludwig von Mises put discontentment at the heart of his theory of economics. It is because men are discontented, Mises argued, that they strive to better themselves, and in so doing, create wealth.[3] The Israelites were not interested in entrepreneurship; they were interested in complaining. They believed that complaining against God's lack of provision for them was an efficient means of humiliating God, thereby persuading Him to provide more goods and services free of charge. They implied that God did not measure up to their expectations. God may have been doing the best He could, but it was clear to the Israelites that they had committed themselves to a God with limited power.

### 3. Ethical Rebellion

God understood what was in their hearts. He understood that this was a rejection of Him. "Because they believed not in God, and trusted not in his salvation" (v. 22), He brought negative sanctions against them.

The psalmist is warning his readers and listeners not to imagine that God is any less than the God of the creation just because He has not yet answered their prayers. He praises God early in this psalm. He says that God did mighty things in the sight of their fathers (v. 12). He divided the sea to let them pass through (v. 13). He led them with a cloud during the day and fire during the night (v. 14). He gave them water out of rocks (v. 15). There was no justification for discontentment regarding God's provision of His people. Complaints against God are a form of rebellion (v. 17).

The psalmist is not just saying that rebellion was common in Israel because of the supposed discrepancy between what the Israelites wanted and what God provided for them. The psalmist is saying that God is capable of providing every need and every want of everyone.

---

3. Ludwig von Mises, *Human Action: A Treatise on Economics* (New Haven, Connecticut: Yale University Press, 1949), ch. 1, Sec. 2.

He is the Creator and therefore the Owner of all the earth. *Discontentment regarding whatever God has provided is a form of rebellion, and it leads to God's negative sanctions in history.* Discontentment against God is not productive. It brings people under judgment; it does not lead to their enrichment.

Complaining was a continuing mistake of the Israelites in the wilderness. They acknowledged that God had provided for them, but they also implied that God had not fulfilled His end of the bargain. He had not sustained them in luxury in the wilderness. So, they kept raising rhetorical questions about God's ability to improve His performance on the job.

The psalmist knew that this attitude is basic to mankind. He wrote this psalm in order to warn men not to indulge in the sins of the forefathers.

## Conclusion

The Israelites in the wilderness provoked God by calling into question His level of commitment to them and His ability to deliver the goods. *They believed that God could be manipulated through guilt. They were incorrect.* They paid a heavy price for this error. "They were not estranged from their lust. But while their meat was yet in their mouths, The wrath of God came upon them, and slew the fattest of them, and smote down the chosen men of Israel" (vv. 30–31). Even then, they did not learn. "For all this they sinned still, and believed not for his wondrous works" (v. 32).

# 20

## CLOSED MOUTHS, CLOSED EARS

*I am the LORD thy God, which brought thee out of the land of Egypt: open thy mouth wide, and I will fill it. But my people would not hearken to my voice; and Israel would none of me.*

PSALM 81:10–11

The theocentric issue here is God as the sanctions-bringer. The psalmist uses a peculiar set of contrasting images: mouth and ears. He says that God would have filled the open mouths of the Israelites if they had listened to Him. Open mouths are filled with food. The text says that God would have actively filled the mouths of His people, had His people listened to him, but they did not listen to Him. The contrast is between the negative sanctions of God and ethical rebellion against the law of God. This is the contrast that Moses revealed in the later sections of Leviticus 26 and Deuteronomy 28.

### A. Honey in the Rock

When the Israelites refused to listen to God, meaning that they refused to obey biblical law, God gave them over to their own lust (v. 12). He refused to intervene to drag them back to ethical conformity to the Mosaic law. So, they walked in their own counsels. They decided which laws to obey or not obey. If they had obeyed God, he says, He would have subdued their enemies and turned His hand against their adversaries (v. 14). He would have given them victory. But, rather than choosing victory, they chose to walk in their own counsels. They preferred to exercise what they perceived as their autonomy.

Then comes a strangely worded revelation. "He should have fed them also with the finest of the wheat: and with honey out of the

87

rock should I have satisfied thee" (v. 16). What is peculiar about this verse is that the psalmist speaks of God in the first clause, and then God speaks as God in the second. The message is consistent. Had they obeyed God, God would have fed them with the finest wheat. To sweeten that wheat, He would have given them honey out of the rock. The phrase, "honey out of the rock," refers back to Deuteronomy. Moses described God's deliverance of Canaan into their hands. He spoke (sang) of Israel in the past tense. This was prophecy, not history. Israel had not yet captured Canaan.

> He made him ride on the high places of the earth, that he might eat the increase of the fields; and he made him to suck honey out of the rock, and oil out of the flinty rock; Butter of kine, and milk of sheep, with fat of lambs, and rams of the breed of Bashan, and goats, with the fat of kidneys of wheat; and thou didst drink the pure blood of the grape. But Jeshurun waxed fat, and kicked: thou art waxen fat, thou art grown thick, thou art covered with fatness; then he forsook God which made him, and lightly esteemed the Rock of his salvation. They provoked him to jealousy with strange gods, with abominations provoked they him to anger. They sacrificed unto devils, not to God; to gods whom they knew not, to new gods that came newly up, whom your fathers feared not (Deut. 32:13–17).

Israel would turn its back on God, Moses said. The psalmist verifies that this had already happened.

### B. Predictable Outcomes

This psalm rests on the ethical cause-and-effect system that is presented in Leviticus 26 and Deuteronomy 28. The psalmist reminds listeners that God is predictable. He is a predictable because He honors the terms of His covenants. His covenants are governed by laws that He has revealed to His covenant people. He enforces these laws by external sanctions. Because He conforms Himself to His covenants, it is possible for covenant-breakers and covenant-keepers to make sense of the world around them (Deut. 4:5–8).[1]

Because God's covenants provide predictability in the social order, people can pursue their goals with confidence that they can attain their goals, just so long as their goals are consistent with God's covenants. If they obey His laws, He will bless their efforts. This makes it possible for them to comprehend social cause and effect. *They can achieve their goals because they understand social cause and effect.*

---

1. Gary North, *Inheritance and Dominion: An Economic Commentary on Deuteronomy*, 2nd ed. (Dallas, Georgia: Point Five Press, [1999] 2012), ch. 8.

The economic goal that is mentioned by the psalmist is related to food. God would have filled their mouths if they had obeyed His law. He would have fed them the best wheat and sweetened it with honey if they had obeyed His Laws. Because they were disobedient, they did not enjoy low-cost, high-quality food. They walked away from wealth. The means of wealth, according to the psalmist, is to hearken to the word of God. If men will listen to God and obey what they hear, they will prosper.

There are still traces of this worldview in folk wisdom. Benjamin Franklin is famous for the phrase, "honesty is the best policy." *Honesty is the best policy because we live in a world governed by biblical law.* God's law repeatedly calls men to honesty. It also says that those who obey biblical law will prosper. This is the unstated theological foundation of Franklin's confident assertion that honesty is the best policy. There is ethical causation in this world.

The covenantal goal of obedience is the extension of the kingdom of God in history. This is why God says that if the Israelites had hearkened to His word, He would have suppressed their enemies. This is another way of saying that He would have extended His kingdom in history. That would have been advantageous to Him, and it would have been advantageous to the Israelites. They would have been the head, and their enemies would have been the tail. This is promised in Deuteronomy 28. "And the LORD shall make thee the head, and not the tail; and thou shalt be above only, and thou shalt not be beneath; if that thou hearken unto the commandments of the LORD thy God, which I command thee this day, to observe and to do them" (Deut. 28:13).[2]

Covenant-keepers can have confidence in the promise of God that He will uphold His people when they are obedient to Him. This is the way to wealth. *We do not live in a world governed by impersonal forces. We live in a world governed by an absolutely sovereign God.*[3] This God covenants with His people, promising them to uphold their cause if they uphold His laws. There is positive feedback between obedience and prosperity. There is also negative feedback between disobedience and poverty. This is why the enemies of God can become the head, and covenant-keepers become the tail. This also is taught in Deuteronomy 28. "He shall lend to thee, and thou shalt not lend to him: he shall be the head, and thou shalt be the tail" (Deut. 28:44).[4]

---

2. *Ibid.*, ch. 70.

3. Gary North, *Sovereignty and Dominion: An Economic Commentary on Genesis* (Dallas, Georgia: Point Five Press, [1982] 2012), ch. 1.

4. North, *Inheritance and Dominion*, ch. 70.

The psalmist upholds the ethical cause-and-effect system that was presented in the Mosaic law. *This psalm makes no sense apart from the Mosaic law*. Anyone in the New Testament era who quotes this psalm, believing that it applies to him and his household, has imported the covenantal structure of the Mosaic law, whether or not he believes that the Mosaic law is still in force. *This psalm and the system of sanctions in Leviticus 26 and Deuteronomy 28 are inseparable*. To attempt to separate them is futile. It would mean invoking this psalm without invoking the system of ethical cause and effect that is presented in Leviticus 26 and Deuteronomy 28. To import this psalm into the New Covenant era, while denying the legitimacy and continuing authority of Leviticus 26 and Deuteronomy 28, is an act of theological schizophrenia.

## Conclusion

The psalmist says that God was ready to feed His people with the best food. They rebelled against Him, so He did not treat them with the degree of favor that He would have shown to them. Moses in his song had prophesied that this would happen. This psalm rests on the presupposition that the corporate sanctions in Leviticus 26 and Deuteronomy 28 are still in force. There is continuity of biblical law and its corporate sanctions. This psalm makes no sense if the sanctions are no longer in force.

# 21

## EXPLOITATION AND
## DELIVERANCE

*A Psalm of Asaph. God standeth in the congregation of the mighty; he judgeth among the gods. How long will ye judge unjustly, and accept the persons of the wicked? Selah. Defend the poor and fatherless: do justice to the afflicted and needy. Deliver the poor and needy: rid them out of the hand of the wicked.*

PSALM 82:1–3

Psalm 82 is a psalm of judgment. The psalmist calls upon God to intervene in the affairs of men and bring justice to the nation.

### A. Civil Magistrates

The psalm begins with a description of God, who stands in the midst of the congregation of the mighty. "He judgeth among the gods." The meaning of *gods* here is *civil magistrates*. The Hebrew word, *elohim*, is usually translated *God* or *gods*. Not in this passage. "I have said, Ye are gods; and all of you are children of the most High. But ye shall die like men, and fall like one of the princes" (Psalm 82:6–7).

God stands in the midst of the judges, and He calls them to account: "How long will ye judge unjustly, and accept the persons of the wicked" (v. 2)? What does it mean "to accept the persons of the wicked"? It means to show partiality to the wicked.

> Ye shall not respect persons in judgment; but ye shall hear the small as well as the great; ye shall not be afraid of the face of man; for the judgment is God's: and the cause that is too hard for you, bring it unto me, and I will hear it (Deut. 1:17).[1]

---

1. Gary North, *Inheritance and Dominion: An Economic Commentary on Deuteronomy*, 2nd ed. (Dallas, Georgia: Point Five Press, [1999] 2012), ch. 4.

91

For the LORD your God is God of gods, and Lord of lords, a great God, a mighty, and a terrible, which regardeth not persons, nor taketh reward (Deut. 10:17).

Thou shalt not wrest judgment; thou shalt not respect persons, neither take a gift: for a gift doth blind the eyes of the wise, and pervert the words of the righteous (Deut. 16:19).[2]

## B. Defend the Poor

Then God issues a command: "Defend the poor and the fatherless: do justice to the afflicted and needy" (v. 3). This was a requirement of the Mosaic law. The Mosaic law recognized that judges sometimes favor one group against another. The Mosaic law forbade judges from rendering judgment that is based on someone's group membership. Each individual case is to be judged in terms of what the law says regarding the accusation. "Ye shall do no unrighteousness in judgment: thou shalt not respect the person of the poor, nor honour the person of the mighty: but in righteousness shalt thou judge thy neighbour" (Lev. 19:15).[3]

Then God says, "Deliver the poor and needy: rid them out of the hand of the wicked" (v. 4). This describes a poor person as being subjected to someone who is breaking the Mosaic law. The hand of the wicked has captured righteous people. The task of civil government is to see to it that justice is done by the rich and the poor to the rich and the poor. These wicked people walk in darkness (v. 3).

The psalmist says, "the foundations of the earth are out of course." This is not to be taken as a statement regarding astrophysics. It is a statement regarding the foundations of morality in Israel. It has to do with the exercise of judgment by covenantal institutions. When judges render false judgment, the earth is ready to be shaken. Of the king of Babylon, Isaiah prophesied:

They that see thee shall narrowly look upon thee, and consider thee, saying, Is this the man that made the earth to tremble, that did shake kingdoms; That made the world as a wilderness, and destroyed the cities thereof; that opened not the house of his prisoners? (Isa. 14:16–17)

The foundations are not literal, any more than God's nose is literal.

Then the earth shook and trembled; the foundations of heaven moved and shook, because he was wroth. There went up a smoke out of his nostrils,

---

2. *Ibid.*, ch. 40.
3. Gary North, *Boundaries and Dominion: An Economic Commentary on Leviticus*, 2nd ed. (Dallas, Georgia: Point Five Press, [1994] 2012), ch. 14.

and fire out of his mouth devoured: coals were kindled by it. He bowed the heavens also, and came down; and darkness was under his feet. And he rode upon a cherub, and did fly: and he was seen upon the wings of the wind (II Sam. 22:8–11).

The psalmist says, "Arise, O God, judge the earth: for thou shalt inherit all nations" (v. 8). This is a call for God to exercise His sovereignty in history. The justification of this exercise of sovereignty is that He is the inheritor of the nations. The nations belong to God. He is their creator, and so He has the right of inheritance.

The psalmist speaks in the name of God. God calls the judges to render judgment righteously. The complaint is against the judges. This psalm is about civil judgment. This is why the references to the need for defense of the poor and fatherless are in the context of civil unrighteousness. The civil government has been misusing the power of the state to render judgments that are opposed to basic morality. These judgments have the force of law. God, who brings covenant lawsuits against covenant-breakers, calls the judges of Israel to render judgment righteously, without respect to persons.

## Conclusion

This is not a psalm that favors wealth redistribution from the poor to the rich. It favors wealth redistribution from those who have misused the civil government to exploit the poor. Their victims are to be compensated. It is a call on civil judges to deliver the victims of oppression. Oppression in the Mosaic law involved the misuse of civil law to afflict people.[4]

*→ Wealth redistribution from those who have misused the civil government to exploit the poor.*

---

4. Gary North, *Authority and Dominion: An Economic Commentary on Exodus* (Dallas, Georgia: Point Five Press, 2012), Part 3, *Tools of Dominion* (1990), ch. 48.

## 22

## A LAND FOR GOD'S LAW

*And gave them the lands of the heathen: and they inherited the labour of the people; That they might observe his statutes, and keep his laws. Praise ye the LORD.*

PSALM 105:44–45

### A. Canaan as Israel's Inheritance

The psalmist calls Canaan an inheritance. It was an inheritance through disinheritance. This is the theocentric issue.

The psalmist refers to the inheritance of the labor of the people. He did not mean that they would inherit labor in the form of slaves. On the contrary, they were not supposed to take any slaves of the people of the land. Only because the Gibeonites deceived them, and only because Israel's civil rulers made a covenant with the Gibeonites in the name of God, did God allow the Gibeonites to remain in the land (Josh. 9). So, the psalmist was speaking of *capital goods*: vineyards, orchards, buildings, and tools. This indicates that he understood what modern economists have insisted on, namely, that *capital is the product of land plus labor over time.*[1]

The labor which the Canaanites had invested in the land produced capital. This capital became the property of the Israelites. This was their inheritance. It was an inheritance transferred by violence. It was the lawful and ethically mandatory transfer of what the Canaanites had intended to be their inheritance. God disinherited the Canaanites by means of extermination. Everything they had built in the name of their gods was to be transferred to the Israelites in the name of their God.

---

1. Murray N. Rothbard, *Man, Economy, and State: A Treatise on Economic Principles*, 2nd ed.(Auburn, Alabama: Mises Institute, [1962] 2009), ch. 5:4.

This is the model for the final judgment. *The final transfer of the inheritance is by violence.* This is the ultimate violence. "And death and hell were cast into the lake of fire. This is the second death. And whosoever was not found written in the book of life was cast into the lake of fire" (Rev. 20:14–15).

### B. Confiscation in the Name of God

The psalmist says that God gave them the lands of the heathen. Yet we also know that they confiscated the lands of the heathen. This confiscation by military violence was authorized by God. He gave them the land, but the means by which they extended their dominion over the land was military. The conquest generation was told to exterminate every heathen in the land.

> When the LORD thy God shall bring thee into the land whither thou goest to possess it, and hath cast out many nations before thee, the Hittites, and the Girgashites, and the Amorites, and the Canaanites, and the Perizzites, and the Hivites, and the Jebusites, seven nations greater and mightier than thou; And when the LORD thy God shall deliver them before thee; thou shalt smite them, and utterly destroy them; thou shalt make no covenant with them, nor shew mercy unto them: Neither shalt thou make marriages with them; thy daughter thou shalt not give unto his son, nor his daughter shalt thou take unto thy son. For they will turn away thy son from following me, that they may serve other gods: so will the anger of the LORD be kindled against you, and destroy thee suddenly. But thus shall ye deal with them; ye shall destroy their altars, and break down their images, and cut down their groves, and burn their graven images with fire. For thou art an holy people unto the LORD thy God: the LORD thy God hath chosen thee to be a special people unto himself, above all people that are upon the face of the earth (Deut. 7:1–6).

Anyone else remaining in the land was there only because the Israelites failed to do the job of confessional cleansing. It is clear in the Old Testament that God required this. Confessional cleansing was not an option; it was a command directly from God. They were to make no covenants of any kind with them, including a peace treaty. Only by deception did the Gibeonites successfully arrange a treaty with the Israelites. The price of that treaty was permanent servitude of the entire nation of the Gibeonites. They served as temple servants, cutting wood and carrying water (Josh. 9:3–17). Joshua announced to them,

> Now therefore ye are cursed, and there shall none of you be freed from being bondmen, and hewers of wood and drawers of water for the house

of my God. And they answered Joshua, and said, Because it was certainly told thy servants, how that the LORD thy God commanded his servant Moses to give you all the land, and to destroy all the inhabitants of the land from before you, therefore we were sore afraid of our lives because of you, and have done this thing (Josh. 9:23–24).

This indicates that the Gibeonites fully understood what God planned for all of Canaan. They decided to avoid the looming genocide. They were successful.

### C. Headquarters

The psalmist tells us one reason for giving the Promised Land to the heirs of Abraham. He was establishing a land in which there could be no excuse for anyone who failed to worship the God of the Bible in public places. He was establishing headquarters for the extension of His worldwide kingdom. He was establishing a place where all the people in the land who were covenanted to Him would be allowed to observe His statutes. They would fall under negative civil sanctions for not observing His statutes. God was setting up a theocratic, exclusivist, geographically identifiable region on earth in which He, and He alone, would be worshiped publicly. He was establishing a place in which the heathen would play no covenantal role whatsoever.

There was to be no rival God inside the geographical boundaries of the Promised Land. The inheritance was to be established covenantally under the God of the Bible. He was unwilling to tolerate any rival inheritance in the Promised Land. Only within the households of resident aliens could another god be worshiped. This is never stated in the Mosaic law, but it is clear that certain resident aliens, called in Hebrew *nokree*, were not covenant-keepers. They were not allowed to proselytize. But there is no indication that God authorized the civil government to bring sanctions inside the households of resident aliens regarding their worship. This worship had to stay inside their households. Even here, I am making the supposition only on the basis of silence. There is no law found in the Mosaic law that would give the state the right to enter the homes of covenant-breakers and execute them for worshiping a God that they had not been publicly forced to renounce when moving into the Promised Land.

The modern world, including modern Christianity, finds this story of genocide an embarrassment—a stain on the covenantal inheritance. But there was a reason for genocide. The reason is given in verse 45. "The land was given to them by God that they might observe his statutes and keep his laws." So important was it to God that the Israelites keep His laws that He commanded them to exterminate everybody in Canaan, without mercy, in order to clear the judicial decks. This command, if obeyed, would reduce the likelihood that the Israelites would be lured into worshiping foreign gods inside what had been the land of Canaan.

God wanted an absolute monopoly over the legal system of Israel. To gain this monopoly, He told the Israelites that they had to exterminate all of the Canaanites, tear down all of the idols, and not worship the gods of the land. God was so jealous about Himself that He tolerated no other legal order inside the boundaries of the Promised Land.

By adhering to the Mosaic law inside Israel, the Israelites were supposed to develop mastery of God's tool of dominion: biblical law. They were to master the biblical art of *casuistry*: the application of the Ten Commandments and the case laws of Exodus[2] to specific situations. Under the Old Covenant order, this required a monopoly over the civil law. The land of Israel was to become a kind of judicial laboratory for biblical law. The experiment failed because of the Israelites' lack of faith. This began at the time of the conquest.

> Yet the children of Manasseh could not drive out the inhabitants of those cities; but the Canaanites would dwell in that land. Yet it came to pass, when the children of Israel were waxen strong, that they put the Canaanites to tribute; but did not utterly drive them out (Josh. 17:12–13).

After Israel's return from captivity, they never again were called by God to extend His kingdom through military conquest. They never again had control over civil law as an independent nation.

## Conclusion

The issue here is inheritance. Biblical inheritance is to be comprehensive, universal, and exclusive. This refers to the final judgment in the final inheritance/disinheritance. But, over time, progressive sanctification is will lead to the extension of the kingdom of God in history. This kingdom will extend God's influence in history into every area of life. Wherever sin reigns, the gospel will invade. There are no sanctuaries for covenant-breaking in the New Testament.

There is no exclusive geographical kingdom of God in the New Testament. There is no place of refuge, no sanctuary, that is exclu-

---

2. Gary North, *Authority and Dominion: An Economic Commentary on Exodus* (Dallas, Georgia: Point Five Press, 2012), Part 3, *Tools of Dominion* (1990).

sively governed by God and His people. The inheritance is supposed to be gained by means of evangelism. The goal is to bring cove-nant-keepers to saving faith in Jesus Christ, thereby appropriating their inheritance in the name of the God of the Bible. Inheritance and this inheritance are confessional issues. There is no comparable inheritance given by means of military action in the New Covenant.

# 23

# LEAN-SOULED PEOPLE

*And he gave them their request; but sent leanness into their soul.*

PSALM 106:15

God is the judge. These words are among the most powerful in the Bible. The psalmist describes the spiritual condition of the Israelites immediately following their deliverance from the Egyptians at the Red Sea. For a brief time, they saw what God had done, and they trusted in His words. "And the waters covered their enemies: there was not one of them left. Then believed they His words; they sang his praise" (vv. 11–12). In the next verse, the psalmist says that they lost all recollection of His works. As a result, they ceased to wait on His counsel (v. 13).

## A. The Demand for More

They departed from faith and adopted rebellion. They "lusted exceedingly in the wilderness, and tempted God in the desert" (v. 14). These were discontented people. They continually asked God for more. They had adopted the religion described by Jesus as the religion of Mammon (Matt. 6:24–25).[1] The confession of faith of the followers of Mammon is this: "More for me in history." With this as background, we can better understand the words of the psalmist: "He gave them their request; but sent leanness into their soul."

This description of the followers of Mammon is applicable in every culture in history. The followers of Mammon are concerned about what they have and what they do not have. What they have never

---

1. Gary North, *Priorities and Dominion: An Economic Commentary on Matthew*, 2nd ed. (Dallas, Georgia: Point Five Press, [2000] 2012), ch. 14.

satisfies them. What they do not have always agitates them. They are obsessed with *more*. By its very nature, *more* cannot be satisfied. It is open-ended. It is a treadmill of discontent leading to greater discontent.

### B. The Price of More

The psalmist describes a contrast. On the one hand, God gave them their request. He gave them more because they asked for more. But He did not give them more at zero price. He sent leanness into their souls. This is another way of saying that, as they became richer in terms of goods, they became poorer in terms of life. The meaning of *soul* in this passage is not confined to that portion of man that survives the death of the body. It is broader than this. It has to do with life itself. The soul in this sense defines the individual. The soul identifies the person's dreams, hopes, priorities, and sense of well-being.

When a person asks himself "How am I doing?" there are two ways of answering this question. First, he can look at what he has accumulated. He can assess how well he is doing by means of success indicators. He can look at the size of his house, the size of his income, the size of his bank account, or the size of his company. In modern America, the single greatest manifestation of great wealth is invisibility from the highway. A person who owns so much urban land that his house is not visible from the street is an extremely wealthy person. Ironically, it is the inability of his neighbors to see how much he possesses that is the mark of a man who possesses great wealth. His servants recognize his wealth; his peers recognize wealth; but the general public does not. The fact that he has servants is also indicative of great wealth. The average person has labor-saving machinery. The wealthy man has labor-saving machinery and a full-time staff to use this machinery in his service.

There is another way of answering the question. When he wants to know how well he is doing, a person focuses on his own soul. He focuses on his sense of accomplishment. He goes to the inner core of his being, and then he assesses the relationship between what he has dreamed about, what he has planned for, what he has worked for, and what he has actually achieved. The psalmist recognizes that an individual can accumulate possessions and nevertheless have a sense of leanness in his soul. Even worse, a person can be so lean in his soul that he does not perceive that his life is a failure. This was Jesus' point in his parable of the rich man who tore down his barns and built new barns to hold all of the grain he expected to accumulate. He died that night. Jesus referred to him as a fool (Luke 12:15–21).[2]

The psalmist says that while the Israelites were granted what they wanted from God, God extracted payment from them by sending leanness into their souls. The psalmist is clear about God as the source of this leanness. It was not that God removed fullness; it was that He sent leanness. God imposed a negative sanction on them. This negative sanction affected the core of their being. Their lives were worth less in direct proportion to their possessions, which were worth more. What they gained in marketable wealth they paid for in a loss of contentment. As they accumulated wealth, they found themselves increasingly dissatisfied. This was the problem of the exodus generation. It began at the time that Moses and Aaron announced God's deliverance. At first, they rejoiced. But as soon as Pharaoh imposed negative sanctions on them for disobedience, the elders of Israel criticized Moses because they believed the Pharaoh would impose additional negative sanctions on them (Ex. 5:21). They did not want deliverance on these terms.

They did not want deliverance on any available terms. They continually complained to Moses that God had brought them into the wilderness to kill them. No matter what God did to demonstrate His care for them, they insisted that He had not done enough. They repeatedly asked: "What have you done for us lately?" They were obsessed by what they perceived as a discrepancy. They overestimated their own importance, and they underestimated the value of their deliverance. Their ability to assess value was crippled.

They were former slaves who were being called on by God to conquer Canaan and build a civilization. This was more than they were prepared to do. So, they wandered for 40 years until they all died off. Only after all of them were dead did God deliver Canaan into the hands of His people. The conquest generation was not the exodus generation.

From the beginning, these people were lean-souled people. Their spiritual condition grew worse as their economic conditions improved. They got what they wanted, but it did them no good. This was what Moses had warned them about. "And thou say in thine heart, My power and the might of mine hand hath gotten me this wealth. But thou shalt remember the LORD thy God: for it is he that

2. Gary North, *Treasure and Dominion: An Economic Commentary on Luke*, 2nd ed. (Dallas, Georgia: Point Five Press, [2000] 2012), ch. 25.

giveth thee power to get wealth, that he may establish his covenant which he sware unto thy fathers, as it is this day" (Deut. 8:17–18).[3]

## Conclusion

There is a price for pursuing and then attaining foolish goals: a lean soul. This comes to someone who confuses success indicators with actual success. He pursues and accumulates the trappings of success, unaware of the fact that these can lure him away from those things that matter most in retrospect at the end of his life. The lean-souled person does not perceive that he is paying for success by accumulating success indicators.

---

3. Gary North, *Inheritance and Dominion: An Economic Commentary on Deuteronomy*, 2nd ed. (Dallas, Georgia: Point Five Press, [1999] 2012), chaps. 21–22.

*"His wonders in the deep"*

# 24

## OVERCOMING FEAR

*They that go down to the sea in ships, that do business in great waters; These see the works of the LORD, and his wonders in the deep.*

PSALM 107:23−24

The theocentric issue here is the sovereignty of God. The psalmist's words introduce a passage dealing with the risks of sailing in the open sea, and God's intervention into the affairs of men to provide protection for them. He singles out seafaring men as people who face the manifestations of God's power regularly.

The King James translators translated the Hebrew word as *business*. More often, the word is translated *work, works,* or *workmanship*. It refers to a group of activities broader than just the conduct of business. Nevertheless, the common work of men who sail the seas is business. Water provides a way for individuals to ship large, bulky, and heavy goods at a relatively low cost per distance traveled. The shipping lanes are filled with ships whose owners seek a profit.

The text says that men who live on the sea or ocean see the works of God. The psalmist speaks of wonders in the deep. He says that God commands the sea, raising the stormy wind. This creates waves (v. 25). The waves are immense, the psalmist says; they rise like mountains and go down again into the depths. Men who sail the sea are fearful whenever storms like this occur. "They reel to and fro, and stagger like a drunken man, and are at their wit's end" (v. 27). At that point, they cry to the Lord in their trouble. God does not ignore their cry. He brings them out of their distresses (v. 28). Then He calms the sea. This was done by Jesus during His ministry as a way to demonstrate His office of Messiah (Matt. 8:23−27).

103

The psalmist says that the men are glad because the waves are quiet. God brings them to their desired haven. Then the psalmist draws a conclusion: "Oh that men would praise the Lord for his goodness, and for his wonderful works to the children of men" (v. 31).[1] This is altogether proper. Their praise of God should be public in the congregation (v. 32).

"He turneth the rivers into a wilderness, and the water springs into the dry ground; a fruitful land into barrenness, for the wickedness of them that dwell therein" (vv. 33–34). Here we see the twofold system of sanctions: positive and negative. It is not that God rewards covenant-keepers, and lets it go at that. It is that he also curses covenant-breakers. Water provides life in the wilderness, and God provides water. Then men sow the fields and plant vineyards. God is the source of the conditions of production. Men then add labor over time.

The psalmist affirms that God is the source of deliverance, because He is also the source of the crisis. He is the source of the gigantic waves that threaten those who go down to the sea in ships. They understand that God is in control of the sea, and therefore they pray to Him. He then intervenes in the affairs of the sea, thereby confirming the faith of those who prayed to Him. Cause and effect are governed by God.

The sovereignty of God is the basis of His control over nature. God is in complete control over nature, and therefore He can be trusted in the affairs of men. He has sufficient power to bring to pass whatever He chooses. The verbal picture here is of the power of the waves to smash ships. God has power over the waves, so the implication is that God is also in control of the ships. Those who believe that God is in control of the waves are in a much better position to have faith in God and to trust the fact that He can deliver them out of their crisis. By giving them confidence in their own efforts, as agents of an absolutely sovereign God, the psalmist raises the standard of performance. Just as God turned the fruitful land into barrenness, so He also turns the wilderness into a standing water, and dry ground into wellsprings. There is a great reversal.

The psalmist says that those who go down to the sea in ships are aware that God is behind the affairs of nature. This gives them an advantage. They can call upon the God who rules over nature to act on their behalf.

1. The psalmist repeats this four times in this psalm.

## Conclusion

The covenant-keeper knows that he does not live in a random, impersonal universe. He is supposed to believe that God is on the side of covenant-keepers. He prays accordingly.

Where this faith is widespread, men take greater chances. They are willing to commit more to their endeavors. They become entrepreneurs because they overcome the supreme barrier to entry: fear. Men who go down to the sea in ships should trust God. This is supposed to keep them doing business.

*They do business — They become entrepreneurs because they overcome the supreme barrier to entry — Fear*

*God is the source of deliverance, because He is also the source of the crisis.*

*1) source of the gigantic waves that threaten whose who go down to the sea in ships*

*2) They understand that God is in control of the sea*

*3) They pray to Him.*

*4) He then intervenes in the affairs of the sea.*

*5) ∴ Confirms the faith of those who pray to Him.*

*Cause & effect are governed by God.*

*The sovereignty of God is the basis of His control over nature.*

# 25

# BUY LOW, SELL HIGH

*He turneth rivers into a wilderness, and the watersprings into dry ground; A fruitful land into barrenness, for the wickedness of them that dwell therein.*

PSALM 107:33—34

## A. Negative Sanctions

The theocentric issue here is God as the sanctions-bringer. There is a famous saying which encapsulates the secret of economic success: buy low, sell high. In this passage, the psalmist describes the scenario known as "buy high, sell low." This is the scenario of negative sanctions. But he also describes another scenario: buy low, sell high. This is the mark of positive sanctions. The psalmist indicates that both patterns are the result of God's intervention into history.

In the first case, the psalmist describes the transformation of plenty into poverty. He says that God turns rivers into a wilderness, and the water springs into dry ground. Without water, land becomes barren. This is how the psalmist describes the results of God's intervention. The fruitful land becomes barren. Why? "For the wickedness of them that dwell therein" (v. 34). Here we see the outworking of the covenantal system of cause and effect that Moses announced to the conquest generation. In Deuteronomy 28:15–68, we find a long list of negative sanctions. These sanctions are imposed by God against covenant-breaking societies. There is a predictable relationship between covenant-breaking and impoverished land. The psalmist appropriates this description, and he applies it to the condition of agricultural land. Water or the absence of water is the determining factor in the productivity of the land. He says that God supplies the water or removes it, according to the owners' ethics.

106

## B. Positive Sanctions

In contrast to God's transformation of productive, well-watered land into wilderness, the psalmist says that God turns the wilderness into standing water, and dry ground into water springs (v. 35). Once the land is improved by the addition of water, God supplies this newly productive land to hungry people (v. 36). Why does He do this? "That they may prepare a city for habitation" (v. 36). To build a city, they need agricultural productivity; therefore, they sow the fields and plant vineyards, which may yield fruits of increase (v. 37). In other words, *out of agricultural productivity will come cities.*

As agriculture becomes more productive, competitive farms reduce the price of the food which they bring to market. They are able to sell all of their output by lowering their prices. City people, who specialize in tasks other than agriculture, can increase their consumption of food simply by paying farmers to sell them their crops. Agricultural surpluses make cities possible. The psalmist understands this principle.

The psalmist says that God multiplies the people. God also protects their cattle. "He blesseth them also, so that they are multiplied greatly; and suffereth not their cattle to decrease" (v. 38). This is the fulfillment of two promises given to Israel in the Mosaic law. "And ye shall serve the LORD your God, and he shall bless thy bread, and thy water; and I will take sickness away from the midst of thee. There shall nothing cast their young, nor be barren, in thy land: the number of thy days I will fulfil" (Ex. 23:25–26).[1]

In the New Covenant, God does not deal with geographical Israel on the basis of direct intervention. What differentiates agricultural productivity today is scientific agriculture, water conservation, and other capital investments. The land's productivity is an outcome of science, technology, and capital. *God's historical sanctions have moved from land to the social order.* Different confessions of faith produce different productivity. Confession, not water, is the central issue.

This conclusion is rejected by humanistic economic theory. Few economists seek to relate theological confession and economic development. It is a blind spot that extends back to the origins of scientific economics, which was born in Great Britain as a reaction to the bloodshed of the Puritan revolt and the Civil War (1642–49), the Interregnum (1649–59), and the restoration of Charles II to the throne

---

1. Gary North, *Authority and Dominion: An Economic Commentary on Exodus* (Dallas, Georgia: Point Five Press, 2012), Part 3, *Tools of Dominion* (1990), ch. 55.

(1660). The economists sought to create a science of wealth that did not rely on a confession of faith, either theological or moral.[2]

## C. The Great Reversal

We see here another example of what I call the great reversal. People who live on productive land see their wealth diminish when God withholds water. He does this to uphold His covenant. He imposes negative sanctions on covenant-breakers. Paralleling this development, God brings water to unprofitable barren land. He does this so that He can plant His people on the land, so that they, in turn, can build cities. God sees agricultural productivity as providing the basis of a growing urban population. "And there he maketh the hungry to dwell, that they may prepare a city for habitation" (v. 36).

The next phase of the great reversal relates to politics. God pours contempt on princes. He causes them to walk in the wilderness (v. 40). Wilderness is the curse, and princes find themselves in the wilderness. There is no productivity in the wilderness. The mark of their downfall is the fact that God leads them into the wilderness. But this is only half the story. God raises up the poor on high from affliction (v. 41). He who is exalted is pulled down; he who is afflicted is raised up. There is no equality in this process; people go from riches to rags, and rags to riches. *This is a process of reversal, not a process of egalitarianism.* Nothing in the Bible points to the equalization of conditions between covenant-keepers and covenant-breakers. They have different destinies.

## Conclusion

God actively intervenes to pull down covenant-breakers and raise up covenant-keepers. He imposes losses on covenant-breakers. Their high-priced land becomes low-priced land. He does the opposite with covenant-keepers. This pattern of ethical cause and effect is presented in Leviticus 26 and Deuteronomy 28. The psalmist relies on these two passages to draw a conclusion: God is the source of agricultural productivity.

2. William Letwin, *The Origins of Scientific Economics* (Cambridge, Massachusetts, MIT Press, 1963).

# 26

## JUDICIAL OPPRESSION

*I will greatly praise the LORD with my mouth; yea, I will praise him among the multitude. For he shall stand at the right hand of the poor, to save him from those that condemn his soul.* **Court room**

PSALM 109:30–31

### A. Corrupt Judges

The theocentric issue of this passage is God as the judge. The context of this verse is a courtroom. The language of the passage indicates that the person is on trial. The Hebrew word, *shafat*, means "to judge." This is how it is translated in most instances in the King James Bible. In this case, it is translated as "condemn." To condemn a person's soul refers here to a courtroom. The Hebrew word for "soul," *nephesh*, means "life" or "breath." It does not refer to the New Testament's concept of a soul that survives physical death (Luke 16:19–31). The judges are not planning to sentence his eternal soul to hell. No Mosaic court had any conception of the court as an agency for imposing eternal sanctions. That prerogative belongs exclusively to God.

God stands beside the defendant, who is poor. He stands at his right hand. In the Old Testament, the right hand was associated with power. "Thy right hand, O LORD, is become glorious in power: thy right hand, O LORD, hath dashed in pieces the enemy" (Ex. 15:6). The right hand was also the hand of man's dependence. "So foolish was I, and ignorant: I was as a beast before thee. Nevertheless I am continually with thee: thou hast holden me by my right hand. Thou shalt guide me with thy counsel, and afterward receive me to glory" (Psalm 73:22–24).

The judges are corrupt. They intend to condemn the poor man,

109

who is unable to defend himself, because he is poor. What are the judges planning to do with the poor person? The language indicates that he is going to be sentenced to death.

This passage does not refer to economic oppression. Social Gospel expositors and their theological allies within evangelical churches tend to focus on the word "poor," and then conclude that the passages relating to poverty and oppression are exclusively dealing with economic oppression. The text does not mention economic oppression. It mentions only that the poor person is on trial for his life. The court is not planning to sentence this person to servitude. It is planning to sentence this person to death.

## B. No Respect for Persons

The person is poor. This puts him at a disadvantage in a courtroom. A corrupt courtroom is marked by the practice of respecting persons. This is condemned by the Mosaic law.

> Ye shall not respect persons in judgment; but ye shall hear the small as well as the great; ye shall not be afraid of the face of man; for the judgment is God's: and the cause that is too hard for you, bring it unto me, and I will hear it (Deut. 1:17).[1]

> Thou shalt not wrest judgment; thou shalt not respect persons, neither take a gift: for a gift doth blind the eyes of the wise, and pervert the words of the righteous (Deut. 16:19).[2]

It is also condemned by the New Testament.

> For there is no respect of persons with God (Rom. 2:11).

> And, ye masters, do the same things unto them, forbearing threatening: knowing that your Master also is in heaven; neither is there respect of persons with him (Eph. 6:9).

> But he that doeth wrong shall receive for the wrong which he hath done: and there is no respect of persons (Col. 3:25).

> But if ye have respect to persons, ye commit sin, and are convinced of the law as transgressors (James 2:9).

Whenever any court shows respect for persons, meaning their social standing, or their importance in the community, or their celebrity

---

1. Gary North, *Inheritance and Dominion: An Economic Commentary on Deuteronomy*, 2nd ed. (Dallas, Georgia: Point Five Press, [1999] 2012), ch. 4.
2. *Ibid.*, ch. 40.

status, or their wealth, the court is oppressive. The court is misusing the God-given monopoly of coercion in order to favor certain members of the community. This means that other members of the community are out of favor. This psalm refers to the poor person. This person is about to become a victim of the court.

The poor man suffers from a lack of social standing. He is no one of any great importance. He is not in a position to receive favorable treatment by a corrupt court. He cannot afford to pay a bribe.

### C. God Intervenes in History

The psalmist says that God intervenes in the proceedings of the court. In some way, God will defend a poor person who is being unjustly accused of a capital crime. This person has his life at stake. The court does not respect God as a person, and therefore it respects important people in the community. The poor man is not an important person. His interests will be sacrificed by the court on behalf of those members of the community who do possess social status.

The psalmist believes that God intervenes in history in such a way that the outcomes of specific court decisions will not conform to the expectations of a corrupt court. The court believes that it is in a position of sovereignty. It does not believe that anything can impede its decisions. It also believes that the outcome of its decision is predictable. It will favor certain members of the community at the expense of other members of the community.

The psalmist says that God intervenes in history in order to thwart the evil intentions of the court. The people who believe that God is blind, or that God is impotent, or that God does not exist will find that things do not turn out as they had planned. This is because God intervenes in history on behalf of the oppressed. In this case, He intervenes on behalf of a poor person.

The text does not say that this person is a covenant-keeper. It says that this person is poor, and there are those who seek his life. God will see to it that the evildoers are thwarted in their attempt to take this person's life. God is a defender of those who are unjustly accused. He can be trusted to uphold His word by enforcing decisions counter to the plans and expectations of covenant-breakers who misuse the courts in order to oppress people without social standing in the community.

This psalm presents God as a just judge. This is a familiar theme in the Bible. God, as the supreme Judge, is supremely just. When earthly judges take a stand against the Bible-revealed law of God in their attempt to thwart the kingdom of God, God intervenes on behalf of those who would otherwise have been destroyed by evildoers. God, as the supreme Judge, upholds justice. He does not forget. He does not ignore evildoing. He does not let courts get away with murder indefinitely.

### Conclusion

The psalmist praises God as a defender of the poor. The psalmist does not indicate that God defends them merely because they are poor. He defends them because they are targets of judicial oppression. Someone seeks the life of the poor man, and God stands as a defense attorney who will uphold the targeted victim.

This verse has nothing to do with the idea of economic oppression. It has to do with judicial oppression.

27

# THE INHERITANCE OF THE HEATHEN

*He hath made his wonderful works to be remembered: the LORD is gracious and
full of compassion. He hath given meat unto them that fear him: he will ever be
mindful of his covenant. He hath shewed his people the power of his works, that
he may give them the heritage of the heathen.*

PSALM 111:4–6

The theocentric issue here is inheritance. The psalmist praises God
because God has given meat to the people who fear Him. The psalmist immediately adds that God will ever be mindful of his covenant.

Here we have in one sentence the promise that God upholds
His covenant by consistently providing positive sanctions to covenant-keepers. The person who fears God receives meat from God.
This proves to the recipient that God is mindful of His covenant. The
psalmist then says that God has showed His people the power of His
works. God has intervened in history in a predictable manner, and
therefore all those who call themselves covenant-keepers should have
confidence in the future. Not to have confidence in the future is to
deny the relevance of this passage.    *Have confidence in the future.*

## A. Who Will Inherit What?

The psalmist says that God will give to His people the heritage of the
heathen (v. 6). Inheritance is inherent in the structure of the biblical
covenant. So is disinheritance.[1] Both are inherent in the progress of
history from the Fall of Adam to the final judgment: the transition

---

1. Ray R. Sutton, *That You May Prosper: Dominion By Covenant*, 2nd ed. (Tyler, Texas:
Institute for Christian Economics, [1987] 1992), ch. 5. Gary North, *Unconditional Surrender: God's Program for Victory*, 5th ed. (Powder Springs, Georgia: American Vision,
[1987] 2010), ch. 5.

113

from wrath to grace. God intervenes in history in such a way that those who profess faith in Him, and who obey His laws, will inherit a legacy: the heritage of the heathen. This passage rests on this assumption: there is ethical cause and effect in history. It states clearly that the future belongs to covenant-keepers.

Psalm 136 records God's deliverance of the Israelites out of Egypt (v. 11). He led them through the wilderness (v. 16). He slew famous kings: Sihon and Og (vv. 19–20). "And gave their land for an heritage: for his mercy endureth for ever: Even an heritage unto Israel his servant: for his mercy endureth for ever" (vv. 21–22). Inheritance involved disinheritance: first Egypt's firstborn, then Pharaoh, then the kings outside Canaan. This is the process of progress. God's kingdom replaces Satan's. It will involve comprehensive disinheritance at the last judgment.

The only way for this progress in history to be thwarted is that, for a time, covenant-keepers refuse to acknowledge the power of God's works in history. Because they refuse to acknowledge the power of God's works in history, they delay the comprehensive transfer of the heritage of the heathen to themselves and their confessional heirs. They do not trust God to do what God says He will do. They do not trust the power of God. In theory, they know that God possesses the power to intervene in history and move the world in a particular direction. At the same time, they deny that God has done this yet in the New Testament era, and they also deny that God will do so in the church's era. In other words, hypothetically speaking, God is all-powerful, but in history, God is self-limited. He is so self-limited with respect to the power of the gospel in history that He will transfer the inheritance of covenant-keepers to covenant-breakers.

Cornelius Van Til specifically taught this view of the future. He said that covenant-breakers will increase their power over the affairs of this world, and will also increase their persecution of covenant-keepers. This process will be brought to an end only when Christ returns in final judgment. He believed that covenant-keeping produces weakness, and covenant-breaking produces power.

> But when all the reprobate are epistemologically self-conscious, the crack of doom has come. The fully self-conscious reprobate will do all he can in every dimension to destroy the people of God. So while we seek with all our power to hasten the process of differentiation in every dimension we are yet thankful, on the other hand, for "the day of grace," the day of undeveloped differentiation. Such tolerance as we receive on the part of the world is due

to this fact that we live in the earlier, rather than in the later, stage of history. And such influence on the public situation as we can effect, whether in society or in state, presupposes this undifferentiated stage of development.[2]

### B. Van Til's Vision

To summarize: as men become more consistent, covenant-breakers will exercise increasing control over society. They will seek out the increasingly defenseless covenant-keepers in order to destroy them. Van Til declared, in effect, "Thank God for inconsistent covenant-breakers today!" In short, he not only rejected what this psalm explicitly teaches, he argued that the opposite is in store for God's people.

While most amillennialists hesitate to declare publicly their acceptance of Van Til's view of the culmination of New Testament history, this is what they really believe. Some of them are more consistent than others in stating the comprehensive pessimism, culturally and historically, of amillennialism.

### C. Covenantal Sanctions

These verses in Psalm 111 assert that God is mindful of His covenant. God brings positive sanctions to those who fear Him. God has visibly demonstrated to His people the power of His works in history. He demonstrates this in order to give them confidence that, in the long run, covenant-keepers will inherit the heritage of the heathen.

This is not an inheritance of earthly capital beyond the final judgment. The heritage of the heathen beyond the final judgment is irrelevant. The only heritage that covenant-keepers will receive in the era after the final judgment is that which they have stored up in history. Jesus was quite clear about this. *The way to build capital in eternity is to give away capital in history*. The way we transfer wealth in history to the world beyond the final judgment is to sacrifice for the kingdom of God in history.

> Lay not up for yourselves treasures upon earth, where moth and rust doth corrupt, and where thieves break through and steal: But lay up for yourselves treasures in heaven, where neither moth nor rust doth corrupt, and where thieves do not break through nor steal: For where your treasure is, there will your heart be also (Matt. 6:19−21).[3]

---

2. Cornelius Van Til, *Common Grace* (1947), reprinted in *Common Grace and the Gospel* (Nutley, New Jersey: Presbyterian & Reformed, 1972), p. 85.

3. Gary North, *Priorities and Dominion: An Economic Commentary on Matthew*, 2nd ed. (Dallas, Georgia: Point Five Press, [2000] 2012), ch. 13.

This post-final judgment inheritance has nothing to do with the heritage of the heathen. The heritage of the heathen is inherited only in history. *The psalmist affirms that covenant-keepers will inherit the heritage of the heathen.* This could not be any more clear. Because of their eschatological system, amillennialists deny the truth of this verse. They either ignore this verse or they reinterpret it to apply only to some kind of internal feel-good inheritance of the heritage of the heathen. While the heathens' heirs retain ownership of their visible heritage, somehow Christians are supposed to think of themselves as heirs of the heritage of the heathen. This makes no sense.

An alternative approach is to argue that God favored covenant-keepers under the Old Covenant, but the New Covenant church is not an heir to such support by God. In the New Testament era, amillennialists believe, there is neutrality or else randomness with respect to society-wide outcomes, or even actual opposition. Meredith G. Kline argued for randomness.

> And meanwhile it [the common grace order] must run its course within the uncertainties of the mutually conditioning principles of common grace and common curse, prosperity and adversity being experienced in a manner largely unpredictable because of the inscrutable sovereignty of the divine will that dispenses them in mysterious ways.[4]

This is a defense of *covenantal unpredictability* in history. He and the theologians who share his view of social causation in history—the overwhelming majority today—do not believe that God's kingdom will expand in history into every area of life, transforming the entire civilization as leaven transforms dough, i.e., the transformation described by Jesus. "Another parable spake he unto them; The kingdom of heaven is like unto leaven, which a woman took, and hid in three measures of meal, till the whole was leavened" (Matt. 13:33).[5]

Here is the amillennialist's view. "The New Covenant church is more self-conscious and consistent than the Old Covenant church; therefore, God has removed positive sanctions for covenantal obedience." *The amillennialist has reversed the system of sanctions affirmed by the psalmist.*

Amillennialism teaches explicitly that covenant-keepers will not inherit the heritage of the heathen. The more consistent amillennialists

---

4. Meredith G. Kline, "Comments on an Old-New Error," *Westminster Theological Journal*, XLI (Fall 1978), p. 184. This essay is a critique of Greg L. Bahnsen's view of theonomy.
5. North, *Priorities and Dominion*, ch. 30.

teach something even more debilitating: the heritage of covenant-keepers will be transferred to covenant-breakers sometime in the future. This will take place either at the Great Tribulation, which supposedly is still in the future, or it will take place after the Great Tribulation. Covenant-keepers are cultural losers in history, while covenant-breakers are cultural winners in history: this is the amillennial position.

If amillennialist pastors were more open about this, preaching it several times a year from their pulpits, they would progressively empty their churches. Only masochists enjoy a steady diet of affirmations that they will fail in history, and if they do not fail personally, then their spiritual heirs will fail. I have called this a ghetto mentality.[6] I have also called this the mentality of a prisoner in a concentration camp. I have referred to a denomination that preaches this consistently as the Barbed Wire Reformed Church.

It is not considered good form among Bible commentators to state things so blatantly, but I prefer the truth to good form. There comes a time when expositors have to lay things on the table. Ideas do have consequences. Eschatology does have implications.[7] *Amillennialism cannot be conformed to these verses.* Amillennialism should therefore either be scrapped, or else our confidence in the reliability of God's word should be scrapped. You cannot logically hold to the plain teaching of these verses and simultaneously hold the view of Christianity's future that is maintained by amillennialism. You must say that the inheritance of the heathen never was transferred to covenant-keepers under the Old Covenant, and it will never be transferred in the New Covenant, either. In short, the psalmist either made a mistake historically or else adopted language that was sure to be misinterpreted as referring to history rather than eternity.

## D. Social Pessimism

Both amillennialism and premillennialism are pessimistic with respect to social transformation.

### 1. Amillennialism

Amillennialists declare a radical discontinuity of covenantal administration, Old Covenant vs. New Covenant. They teach that God's promises to covenant-keepers regarding their future inheritance have

---

6. Gary North, "Ghetto Eschatologies," *Biblical Economics Today* (April/May 1992).

7. Gary North, *Millennialism and Social Theory* (Tyler, Texas: Institute for Christian Economics, 1990).

been completely overthrown by Jesus. We are on our own in the New Covenant. This is why all contributions to social theory by amillennialists invoke natural law. Amillennialists do not believe in the continuing authority of biblical laws and their sanctions. This leaves them at the mercy of covenant-breakers and their competing theories of covenants and sanctions.

For the amillennialist, there is no biblically sanctioned cultural progress in history—no civil or cultural progressive sanctification to match individual progressive sanctification, family progressive sanctification, and ecclesiastical progressive sanctification. Amillennialists are forced to admit that the church progresses, Christian family government progresses, and Christian personal self-government progresses. But civil, social, and cultural life supposedly progresses only in terms of non-biblical standards and sanctions.

Herman Hanko, who was the senior theologian of the tiny Dutch-American denomination, the Protestant Reformed Church, held this view of social progress. Only Satan can grant widespread economic success in history, he taught.

> I was compelled to warn God's people against the spiritual dangers involved in postmillennialism. It is my fervent hope and prayer that those who hold to postmillennialism do not actually promote the kingdom of Antichrist; but Herman Hoeksema was right when somewhere he warned God's people of the spiritual danger involved. It is not inconceivable that, if the saints are looking for a glorious kingdom on earth, they will be tempted to identify the kingdom which Antichrist establishes with the kingdom of Christ. It will be hard enough in that dreadful day to stand for the cause of Christ without putting other spiritual temptations in the way.[8]
>
> I do not doubt that a kingdom of peace, of great plenty, of enormous prosperity and uncounted riches, of beauty and splendor such as the world has never seen, will some day be established. Scripture points us to that. What makes one cringe, however, is that this kingdom is described by Scripture as the kingdom of the beast (read Revelation 13). This makes postmillennial thinking of considerable spiritual dangers.[9]

Equally adamant that long-term economic prosperity is of the devil is the accountant and popular writer of paperback dispensational

8. Herman Hanko, "Response to 'The Other Side' of Postmillennialism," *Standard Bearer* (April 1, 1990), p. 295. Cited by Kenneth L. Gentry, Jr., *He Shall Have Dominion: A Postmillennial Eschatology*, 2nd ed. (Tyler, Texas: Institute for Christian Economics, [1992] 1997), p. 506.
9. Herman Hanko, "The Illusory Hope of Postmillennialism," *Standard Bearer* (Jan. 1, 1990), p. 159. Cited in *ibid.*, pp. 506–7.

eschatology books, Dave Hunt. He wrote two books on this: *Peace, Prosperity, and the Coming Holocaust* (1983) and *Whatever Happened to Heaven?* (1988). I reviewed them in 1992.[10]

This outlook implies that social success on a broad base is the result of the creative work of Satan. Satan has overcome the inherent tendency of the social world of the Mosaic law, in which covenant-keepers experience success, while covenant-breakers experience failure. While this was built into the Old Covenant, Van Til, Hanko, and Hunt have insisted that not only has this system of ethical causation been annulled, it has been reversed in the New Testament. In our era, covenant-keeping produces widespread poverty, while covenant-breaking produces widespread prosperity. This prosperity lures unsuspecting and naive covenant-keepers into accepting as legitimate the social goal of long-term economic growth, these authors have argued.

## 2. *Premillennialism*

Premillennialists are as pessimistic as amillennialists with respect to the premillennial age. Premillennialists believe that history will include a millennial victory for Christ, but only because Christ is physically present to give directions to an international bureaucracy of His covenant-keeping people, who will be in charge all over the world.

Premillennialists do not say whether they believe that a centralized hierarchy is the proper form of government for the millennial era. For the most part, they teach that local churches should be sovereign and independent. Presbyterian premillennialists teach that any hierarchical Court of appeals within ecclesiastical circles should be limited. In other words, with respect to the premillennial era, they believe in bottom-up civil government and ecclesiastical government. On the other hand, from the point of view of their view of the millennial era, they are silent.

Premillennialists do not write books on social theory. They do not describe civil and church government after the return of Christ. This has been true for two millennia, so this is not absent-mindedness. *They have nothing to say about church and state in the millennial era.* Premillennial Baptists who believe in local church autonomy do not deal with these two questions:

> How will local churches get Jesus to intervene personally, dispute by dispute, if there are no hierarchical church courts?

10. North, "Ghetto Eschatologies," *op. cit.*

How will Jesus avoid long lines, as described in Exodus 18: the lines in front of Moses' tent?

There are only so many hours in the day, and there will be millions of disputes per year.

Silence in the face of the simplest institutional questions reveals a lack of curiosity on a stupendous scale. Premillennialists do not discuss whether there will be judicial and institutional continuity between the church age and the millennial age. They have no suggestions with respect to the reform of social institutions or the economy in the church age, precisely because they think that the church age favors covenant-breakers and penalizes covenant-keepers.

They are pessimistic with respect to the church age. Their pessimism is matched by the amillennialists' pessimism. Both groups compete with one another on the basis of saying how bad the Great Tribulation is going to be.

The post-tribulation dispensationalist and the historic premillennialist share the view with amillennialism that the church will go through the Great Tribulation. This is one reason why pre-tribulation dispensationalism is popular. It teaches that the church will not go to the tribulation; only the Jews will go through the tribulation. The Jews will be almost completely annihilated: two-thirds.[11]

## E. Risk-Taking

Whenever Christians believe that God brings negative sanctions against them for covenant-keeping—obeying biblical law—they are far less willing to launch high-risk ventures in any area of life. People who take great risks believe there is a possibility of great rewards. When a person is told, from his youth to his deathbed, that the efforts of Christians to extend the kingdom of God in history will come to naught, culturally speaking, they are less willing to commit exceptional time and money to dead-end projects that cannot succeed. It is not just that there are supposedly heavy odds against the success of

11. Gary DeMar, "Dispensationalism's Predicted Jewish Holocaust" (2008). Pre-tribulation dispensationalists often work hard to bring Jews back to Palestine. Why? They believe that Israel will be surrounded during the Great Tribulation and be almost annihilated. Why bring Jews back to Palestine, where it will be more convenient for Satan and his evil rulers on earth to get revenge on the Jews during the Great Tribulation? This is a much more efficient system for destroying the Jews than to warn Jews not to come back Palestine, but remain wherever they are. See Gary North, "Fundamentalism's Bloody Homeland for the Jews" (Nov. 1, 2003): lewrockwell.com/north/north222.html (accessed January 16, 2021).

their projects. There are consistent, highly developed eschatologies that teach that there is absolutely no possibility in history that these projects will come to cultural fruition. There will only be the survival of a besieged little remnant of faithful believers, who will face the combined power of Satan and his dominion, until at the last day, Jesus comes to rescue them, either at the final judgment (amillennialism) or just before the Rapture (pre-tribulational dispensationalism), or just before the millennium (non-dispensational premillennialism and post-tribulational dispensationalism).

*This outlook is the theological foundation of cultural despair.* There are some theologians who revel in this cultural despair. They proclaim it as the highest form of theological wisdom.[12] The only amillennial churches that successfully grow in these circumstances are those in which the pastors ignore or avoid the inescapable implications of their theological position. They do not preach it. They are careful not to remind their listeners of what amillennialism teaches concerning the future.

This can also be said of premillennialists. The same pessimism applies to the era prior to the second coming of Christ to set up an earthly millennium. The church is seen as utterly impotent to change culture, to affect the transformation of civilization, or to reverse the march into Satanic nihilism. Only Jesus can do this, and He will do it only in person. This is the teaching of all premillennialism, not just dispensationalism.

## Conclusion

The psalmist says that there is a covenantal system of inheritance in history. The process of inheritance in history leads to the transfer of the inheritance of the heathen to the sons of God. God upholds His covenant. He gives meat to those who fear Him. The psalmist believed this. Premillennialists and amillennialists do not believe it.

The Great Tribulation is behind us.[13] The inheritance of the heathen's inheritance is in front of us. Let us work accordingly.

---

12. In my day, David J. Engelsma is a good example. He is a theologian of the Protestant Reformed Church. See his editorial, "Jewish Dreams," *The Standard Bearer* (Jan. 15, 1995). Cf. Engelsma, "A Defense of Reformed Amillennialism (I): An Introduction," *Reformed Witness*, IX (July 2001).

13. David Chilton, *The Great Tribulation* (Tyler, Texas: Dominion Press, [1987] 1997).

# 28

# OBEDIENCE AND WEALTH

*Praise ye the* LORD. *Blessed is the man that feareth the* LORD, *that delighteth greatly in his commandments. His seed shall be mighty upon earth: the generation of the upright shall be blessed. Wealth and riches shall be in his house: and his righteousness endureth for ever.*

PSALM 112:1–3

## A. Biblical Law and Personal Blessing

The theocentric issue here is the relationship between law and sanctions. I regard this passage as the most clear-cut statement in the Bible regarding the ethical cause-and-effect relationship between personal covenant-keeping and personal riches. The mark of covenant-keeping is explicitly stated here: delight in the commandments of God.

The passage begins with point one of the biblical covenant: the fear of the Lord. We are to fear God because He is absolutely sovereign. God's sovereignty is point one.[1] The text moves to point four: sanctions.[2] Blessed is the man who fears God. How does the psalmist define fear? By means of a biblical law: point three.[3] The man who fears God is a person who delights greatly in God's commandments. The text does not say "blessed is the man who fears the Lord and who delights in natural law." It does not say that he delights in positive law: state-made law. It surely does not say that he delights in post-

---

1. Ray R. Sutton, *That You May Prosper: Dominion By Covenant*, 2nd ed. (Tyler, Texas: Institute for Christian Economics, [1987] 1992), ch. 1. Gary North, *Unconditional Surrender: God's Program for Victory*, 5th ed. (Powder Springs, Georgia: Point Five Press, [1980] 2010), ch. 1.
2. *Ibid.*, ch. 4. North, ch. 4.
3. *Ibid.*, ch. 3. North, ch. 4.

modernism: law for himself alone. It says that he delights greatly in God's commandments. Where do we find these commandments? In Psalm 119, they are identified: biblical law.

The previous psalm had ended with this affirmation: "The fear of the LORD is the beginning of wisdom: a good understanding have all they that do his commandments: his praise endureth for ever" (Psalm 111:10). The Book of Proverbs affirm that wisdom is the supreme asset to pursue.

> Get wisdom, get understanding: forget it not; neither decline from the words of my mouth (Prov. 4:5).

> Wisdom is the principal thing; therefore get wisdom: and with all thy getting get understanding (Prov. 4:7).

> How much better is it to get wisdom than gold! and to get understanding rather to be chosen than silver! (Prov. 16:16)

The psalmist indicates here that the starting point of wisdom, the fear of the Lord, is manifested through conformity to His law. Then comes wealth.

## B. Blessings Galore

In what does the blessing consist? "His seed shall be mighty upon the earth: the generation of the upright shall be blessed" (v. 2). The blessing comes in the form of familistic blessings. A man's seed, meaning his heir, is mighty upon the earth. This is a person whose family has influence.

It goes beyond his family's influence. The individual who has great fear of the Lord and who delights in His commandments will be a rich man. When the text says "wealth and riches," it does not mean spiritual wealth and spiritual riches. The language of the Psalms is concrete. This text is adamant: *the covenant-keeper who fears God will possess riches*. Furthermore, his righteousness endures forever. Whatever he does to benefit the kingdom of God extends through history. It has influence down through the ages.

Obviously, this passage did not apply to the earthly ministry of Jesus Christ. The Messiah was not a rich man. The Messiah was promised to be a man who suffered persecution (Isa. 53). *But the Messiah's life is not the model that covenant-keepers are supposed to use.* Their model is the man in Psalm 112:3. This is a man who possesses wealth and riches. His influence will expand down through history. What more can someone ask for? Men seek wealth, influence, and fame. This man, who fears the Lord and who delights in God's law, possesses all three.

*The tendency towards wealth is inherent in obeying God's law.* This psalm makes this point as clearly as any text in the Bible. It is *not random* that this individual possesses wealth and riches. He possesses wealth and riches, the text says, because he fears God. The mark of his fear of God is his delight in God's law.

Modern Christians sing a familiar hymn with this chorus: "O how love I thy law. It is my meditation all the day." I cannot think of any hymn as widely sung and less believed. To the extent that modern Christians ever hear a sermon on biblical law, they are told in no uncertain terms that they are *not* under biblical law. They do not hear sermon after sermon, week after week, on what the Mosaic law requires in every area of life. They are not encouraged to read the Mosaic law. They are not encouraged to obey the Mosaic law. They may get an occasional sermon on the Ten Commandments, but they do not get sermons on the case laws of Exodus,[4] the laws of Leviticus,[5] and the laws of Deuteronomy.[6] They are completely ignorant of these books in Scripture. Why is this the case? Because pastors refuse to preach on biblical law. They do not believe in biblical law. They believe in natural law theory, or they believe in some sort of humanistic government-mandated law, but they do not believe in the authority of Bible-revealed law.

Because they do not believe in biblical law, they do not preach obedience to it. Yet they read in texts such as this one that obedience to biblical law brings personal success. If pastors preached regularly on the basis of personal success, including wealth, they would have to confront the issue of obedience to biblical law. *They do not choose to confront this issue, so they do not preach about wealth and success.*

### C. Positive Confession Christianity

There is a group of fundamentalist Christians, sometimes called positive confession, sometimes called "name it and claim it," who do preach about God's standard: wealth. This text and other Old Covenant passages make it clear that *wealth really is God's standard*. It is

---

4. Gary North, *Authority and Dominion: An Economic Commentary on Exodus* (Dallas, Georgia: Point Five Press, 2012), Part 3, *Tools of Dominion* (1990).

5. Gary North, *Boundaries and Dominion: An Economic Commentary on Leviticus*, 2nd ed. (Dallas, Georgia: Point Five Press, [1994] 2012).

6. Gary North, *Inheritance and Dominion: An Economic Commentary on Deuteronomy*, 2nd ed. (Dallas, Georgia: Point Five Press, [1999] 2012).

supposed to be a positive sanction for obedience to biblical law. But positive confession pastors do not preach biblical law. They are as hostile to the Mosaic law as their fellow pastors in other branches of the church. So, they preach wealth in the name of personal spiritual intensity in believing what is not yet visibly true. They tell poor people to believe that they can be rich and that they should be rich. They do not preach that it is their listeners' requirement to restructure their lives in terms of biblical law. They do not preach the necessity of a complete transformation of one's habits as the foundation of wealth. Instead, they preach that people merely need to *believe* that they will become wealthy, and they *really will* become wealthy.

This is a baptized version of what is sometimes called "think and grow rich." It is promoted by science-of-mind advocates and other representatives of non-Christian faiths. In the mid-1950s, there was a best-selling American book titled *The Power of Positive Thinking*. It was written by Rev. Norman Vincent Peale. Rev. Peale was a member of an officially Calvinist denomination, the Reformed Church of America, but his doctrines had nothing to do with Calvinism or the Bible.

### D. Positive Judicial Sanctions

Wealth is supposed to be a confirmation of conformity to God's covenant (Deut. 8:18).[7] Wealth is a positive sanction that God brings on people who delight in His law and who obey it. Wealth is not a blessing whenever it comes on the basis of anything other than covenantal conformity to God's law. Otherwise, it can be a deadly deception. It persuades individuals to believe that they are blessed of God when in fact they are on a slippery slope to perdition. This is taught specifically in Psalm 73.[8]

Because modern Christians are antinomian in their view of the Mosaic law, and because they do not believe in the New Covenant predictability of the specific sanctions attached to the supposedly defunct Mosaic law, *they do not believe in an ethical cause-and-effect universe*. They do not believe that if they conform to biblical law, they will receive positive blessings, including greater wealth. They have been told that this cause-and-effect relationship is no longer operational, although it was operational in theory under the Mosaic Covenant.

Without positive sanctions to confirm their confession of faith and their success in conforming to the laws of God, Christians search

---

7. North, *Inheritance and Dominion*, ch. 22.
8. Chapter 17.

for other forms of verification or confirmation. They want to know that they are on the right track. So, they search for internal blessings. They are told that any search for visible, external blessings is somehow illegitimate. Spiritual feelings of joy replace specifics of God's law and visible wealth. But there is nothing in Psalms about spiritual feelings as valid substitutes for biblical law and wealth.

## Conclusion

The psalmist announces that the man who fears God has an advantage: he is wealthy. His family has influence. What he does for God's kingdom will have effects down through history. All of these are highly respected positive sanctions in most cultures.

The psalmist's announcement rests on faith in the existence of a cosmos governed by ethical cause and effect. This universe is ruled by a sovereign God who enforces the ethical terms of His covenant. He enforces them by imposing visible sanctions. One of these is wealth.

## CHARITABLE LENDING

*A good man sheweth favour, and lendeth: he will guide his affairs with discretion.*

PSALM 112:5

The theocentric issue here is grace. This is an aspect of sanctions. The psalmist says that a good man shows favor to someone who is in a temporary crisis. He lends to such a person. The psalmist adds that the person will guide his affairs with discretion. The good man is willing to lend. He also shows good judgment in the management of his affairs. This man is unique. He knows how to make money, and he also knows how to give it away. His good management has led to sufficient wealth, so he is in a position to lend money at no interest to people who have fallen on hard times.

### A. A Unique Ability

The ability to manage your affairs so that you gain wealth, when coupled with the ability to perceive when another person is in need through no fault of his own, is a unique ability. There are some people who have a gift for making a great deal of money. There are other people who have a gift for giving away money without causing harm. Rarely are these abilities found in the same person. There is specialization of labor in life, and these two specializations seem opposed to each other. If a person is good at making money, he does not want to surrender any of his money, because his chief ability is to multiply what he already owns. If he gives away a portion of his wealth, that portion will not multiply under his administration.

The psalmist insists that the ability to manage your affairs well involves the ability to make accurate judgments about giving away a portion of your wealth. The different skills of making money and the skills of giving away money, when combined in one person, are the model of Christian stewardship. A person who is a good manager of his affairs is confident that, when it comes to wealth, there is more where that came from. He therefore does not fear the loss of revenue that he could otherwise have made by lending money in a commercial loan. He does not mind giving up the forfeited interest in a charitable loan. That income would have been minimal anyway. Compared to the blessings of God on a well-managed household, the forfeited interest on a charitable loan is next to nothing.

The psalmist affirms that a good man shows favor by lending money. He is speaking of a charitable loan.

## B. A Zero-Interest Loan

In the Mosaic Covenant, a charitable loan paid no interest. "Thou shalt not lend upon usury to thy brother; usury of money, usury of victuals, usury of any thing that is lent upon usury. Unto a stranger thou mayest lend upon usury; but unto thy brother thou shalt not lend upon usury: that the LORD thy God may bless thee in all that thou settest thine hand to in the land whither thou goest to possess it" (Deut. 23:19–20).[1] It was morally mandatory for a man with money to lend to a poor brother.

> If there be among you a poor man of one of thy brethren within any of thy gates in thy land which the LORD thy God giveth thee, thou shalt not harden thine heart, nor shut thine hand from thy poor brother: But thou shalt open thine hand wide unto him, and shalt surely lend him sufficient for his need, in that which he wanteth. Beware that there be not a thought in thy wicked heart, saying, The seventh year, the year of release, is at hand; and thine eye be evil against thy poor brother, and thou givest him nought; and he cry unto the LORD against thee, and it be sin unto thee. Thou shalt surely give him, and thine heart shall not be grieved when thou givest unto him: because that for this thing the LORD thy God shall bless thee in all thy works, and in all that thou puttest thine hand unto (Deut. 15:7–10).

The psalmist adds this promise of a positive sanction: "He hath dispersed, he hath given to the poor; his righteousness endureth for ever; his horn shall be exalted with honour" (v. 9). Gaining honor is a way to annoy the wicked. "The wicked shall see it, and be grieved;

---

1. Gary North, *Inheritance and Dominion: An Economic Commentary on Deuteronomy*, 2nd ed. (Dallas, Georgia: Point Five Press, [1999] 2012), ch. 57.

he shall gnash with his teeth, and melt away: the desire of the wicked shall perish" (v. 10).[2]

The psalmist is not speaking of an economic decision to lend money at interest in a commercial venture. Lending money at interest for a commercial venture was legitimate under the Mosaic law. We know this because a person who fell into debt or poverty could be sold into slavery to a stranger in the land. He could be forced to serve for up to 49 years (Lev. 25:47–48).[3] A failure to repay a commercial loan was a reason for servitude. In contrast, the failure to repay a charitable loan was up to six years of slavery (Lev. 25:1–2).

Lending money at interest to covenant-breakers was not only legitimate, it was a mark of God's favor on the lender. God encouraged His people to lend to covenant-breakers. "For the LORD thy God blesseth thee, as he promised thee: and thou shalt lend unto many nations, but thou shalt not borrow; and thou shalt reign over many nations, but they shall not reign over thee" (Deut. 15:6). This was a way of exercising dominion over them.[4] "The LORD shall open unto thee his good treasure, the heaven to give the rain unto thy land in his season, and to bless all the work of thine hand: and thou shalt lend unto many nations, and thou shalt not borrow" (Deut. 28:12).[5] This kind of loan is not what the psalmist is talking about in this verse. He is talking about a morally mandatory charitable loan which paid no interest.

To lend at no rate of interest is a form of charity.[6] Surrendering use over a present good in exchange for a promise to return that good or a comparable good in the future is an exchange of a better condition for a worse condition. *Present goods are worth more to us than the promise of future goods is.* We have the present goods; we do not have the future goods. We enjoy the use of present goods; we do not enjoy the use of future goods. This is why borrowers must promise to pay more in return than they receive as a loan. This is the origin of interest.[7]

---

2. Chapter 30.

3. Gary North, *Boundaries and Dominion: An Economic Commentary on Leviticus*, 2nd ed. (Dallas, Georgia: Point Five Press, [1994] 2012), ch. 31.

4. North, *Inheritance and Dominion*, ch. 37.

5. *Ibid.*, ch. 70.

6. An exception took place in the United States in December 2008. The interest rate on 90-day United States Treasury bills fell to zero on three different days. This sacrifice of interest was a payment for perceived security: the guaranteed return of the money. Fear over bank failures had increased the public's perception that large deposits might not be returned.

7. Ludwig von Mises, *Human Action: A Treatise on Economics* (New Haven, Connecticut: Yale University Press, 1949), ch. 19.

In the case of a charitable loan, the lender is prohibited from accepting interest in any form from a poor fellow covenant member. He therefore surrenders a present good for the promise of a return of a comparable future good. He forfeits the use of the good in the interim. This is a form of charity. This is required by God. Covenant-keepers are told to lend money to covenant-keepers who are in a crisis through no fault of their own. This is a form of social insurance in a covenant community. People who get into temporary trouble know that they can receive zero-interest loans to help them recover.

### Conclusion

The psalmist equates an open hand with wise stewardship. It is not a question of one or the other. The biblical model involves both skills.

# 30

# THE WICKED WILL
## MELT AWAY

*He hath dispersed, he hath given to the poor; his righteousness endureth for ever; his horn shall be exalted with honour. The wicked shall see it, and be grieved; he shall gnash with his teeth, and melt away: the desire of the wicked shall perish.*

PSALM 112:9–10

The theocentric issue here is God's judgment in history, as reflected in the common judgment of men. This is a mark of success. The psalmist describes the activities of the righteous person. This person has dispersed, meaning he has given away wealth. The same Hebrew word is used by the author of Proverbs: "There is that **scattereth**, and yet increaseth; and there is that withholdeth more than is meet, but it tendeth to poverty" (Prov. 11:24).[1] He has given this wealth to poorer people. The psalmist identifies charity as a mark of a righteous person. He then goes on to say that the righteousness of this person endures forever. "His horn shall be exalted with honor." The reference to horn is not specific. "Horn" can sometimes represent power, as with an animal with horns. At other times, it represents the source of blessings, as in a horn full of oil. At other times, it means proclamation. The sound of horns mobilized the nation (Lev. 23:24).

The psalmist says that the wicked man will see this, and it will grieve him. He is not grieving over the fact that the righteous man gave money to the poor. This may have been done in private. *What grieves the wicked person is that the righteous man is regarded as honorable.* He receives public recognition for his honorable life. This causes the

---

1. Gary North, *Wisdom and Dominion: An Economic Commentary on Proverbs* (Dallas, Georgia: Point Five Press, [2007] 2012), ch. 32.

wicked man to gnash his teeth and melt away. He disappears from the scene. He goes away annoyed, but he goes away.

The contrast is between the righteous person and a wicked person. The righteous person gives away a portion of his wealth. While the psalmist does not say that giving away assets is the immediate source of public honor for the righteous man, he does make the connection between charitable giving and widespread personal recognition. This recognition is visible to the wicked person. This is not something that was done in private. The giving was done in private, but the recognition is public. This indicates that his righteousness is comprehensive. He is not being recognized for his charitable activities. He is being recognized for *his way of life*, which is visible.

The righteous individual gains the advantage of public acceptance. This disturbs the wicked person. He does not want to think that a righteous man is publicly regarded as righteous. The contrast between the honor which the righteous man receives and the dishonor which the wicked man receives is too great for the wicked man to tolerate. He is annoyed, but his annoyance does him no good.

The psalmist paints a picture of a righteous individual who has dispersed a portion of his wealth to the poor. His righteousness endures forever, the psalmist says. This means that *his reputation endures.* The psalmist specifically says this: "his horn shall be exalted with honor." This is a public matter. It is so public that the wicked man is grieved by it. This is not some form of success that was achieved in secret. *This is public success.*

The psalmist says the desire of the wicked shall perish. His hopes and dreams will be cut off, in contrast to the reputation of righteousness and honor which are possessed by a righteous and honorable covenant-keeper. The covenant-breaker's future is cut off; the covenant-keeper's future is forever.

The contrast between the public condition of the righteous and the public condition of the wicked is sharp. It is so sharp that the wicked man is offended by it. He seeks to escape the testimony of his own eyes. He then melts away. This means that he disappears from the public scene. He loses influence.

This is an important passage because it affirms the relationship between covenant-keeping and visible success. One of the goals that most men have is recognition. Another goal is to be remembered. The psalmist says that the righteous man will not only receive recognition, he will receive it on a perpetual basis. Theologically, the reason for this is the imputation of righteousness by God. God does not forget. When God imputes righteousness to an individual, this imputation cannot be rescinded. It is perpetual. According to this passage, the righteous individual is the recipient of perpetual imputation, and this imputation is one of honor. This is not a strictly subjective condition of the righteous person's mind. It is a matter of public confirmation. It is so public that the wicked man resents it.

The psalmist says that the desire of the wicked will perish. That which the wicked man upholds and desires will be overcome by righteousness in history. The process of historical development is covenantal. This is why righteousness produces external blessings, while unrighteousness produces external cursings. This is why the wicked man is said to be offended by the visible success of the righteous person.

According to the psalmist, there is predictable consistency between covenant-breaking and the failure to influence culture. This is not true in every era, but it is true with respect to the influence of the righteous, which is forever. *There is a compounding effect in history: righteousness increases, while wickedness melts away.* The wicked person will perish. He will melt away. This is in contrast to the reputation of the righteous person. The psalmist's declaration rests on a system of covenantal cause and effect. Righteousness produces benefits; unrighteousness produces impotence. The unrighteous person melts away. So does his legacy. "A good man leaveth an inheritance to his children's children: and the wealth of the sinner is laid up for the just" (Prov. 13:22).[2]

### Conclusion

The psalmist affirms that righteousness is rewarded in history. He also affirms that unrighteousness is rewarded with impotence in history. This worldview is in stark contrast to the worldview of both amillennialism and premillennialism. Amillennialism teaches that covenant-keeping produces persecution and visible failure. It also teaches that covenant-breaking produces power and influence. This perspective is categorically denied by these two verses of Scripture. Similarly, premillennialists believe that the gospel's long-term failure in changing culture for the better will be reversed only when Jesus comes again physically in absolute power to run a worldwide kingdom of God.

---

2. North, *Wisdom and Dominion*, ch. 41.

The psalmist is not affirming that the outcome of righteousness and the outcome of wickedness are random. The outcomes are not random. They are favorable to covenant-keepers and unfavorable to covenant-breakers.

# 31

## UPWARD SOCIAL MOBILITY

*He raiseth up the poor out of the dust, and lifteth the needy out of the dunghill;*
*That he may set him with princes, even with the princes of his people.*

PSALM 113:7–8

The psalmist insists that God is sovereign over the economic affairs of men. God exercises power to raise up poor people. He is their deliverer. Their poverty need not be permanent. People can be born into poverty, but they can be raised out of it. The idea that poverty is necessarily inter-generational is incorrect. The psalmist says that *God breaks the cycle of poverty*. So completely does God break the cycle of poverty that a man who had been poor can find himself in the presence of the judicial equivalent of an Old Covenant king. He becomes a trusted counselor. Because the adviser has been raised out of poverty, the ruler trusts his wisdom and advice. This, at least, is the implication of the psalmist's assertion that the poor person will be in the presence of kings.

The story of Saul is a story of obscure man lifted up to the kingship. The story of David is much the same. God used Samuel to anoint both Saul and David on His behalf. God picked these men to serve as kings over Israel. Saul was a tall man, and looked like a king should look (I Sam. 9:2), but he had no particular leadership abilities to be king. God nevertheless raised him up out of obscurity to lead the nation of Israel.

The psalmist says that God does not place a social ceiling on the poor man. God has endowed the poor man to perform well enough to impress kings. God overcomes all of the barriers that would otherwise keep a person from entering the court of a king. An individual's talents are the limits on his success. Limits of social tradition, personal connections, formal education, and all of the other barriers to entry mean nothing to God, and should mean nothing to those whom God has picked to represent His position in the courts of kings.

The picture here is *a society with open entry to markets*. Men of talent who gain information of how markets work are authorized by God to continue to improve their skills, master the markets, and gain all the money they can in a voluntary society. The productivity of an individual is not limited by barriers to social entry. God raises up the individual for His own glory, and the individual is put in charge of decision-making. This is the picture in Jesus' parable of the stewards. When the owner of the property returns and demands an accounting, some of the servants turn out to be very productive, but one servant does not. God brings that person under judgment (Matt. 25:14–31).[1]

This is the familiar story of rags to riches. It was not always familiar. The suggestion that God raises up poor men to sit with kings was not familiar in the ancient world. It was a revolutionary suggestion. Even today, this degree of mobility is rare, although it is considered possible in theory. The West's acceptance of this degree of social mobility took centuries to achieve, but from the mid-seventeenth century until today, the ideal of upward social mobility has been basic to the democratic West. This outlook first became common during Cromwell's revolt against King Charles I. His New Model Army contained thousands of men who held such views, most notably the Levelers. These were democrats, not communists. The communists were the Diggers, and they had few representatives in Cromwell's army.

### Conclusion

A society that allows individuals to rise economically, which does not put legal barriers against successful individuals to enter into social contact with others, is a free society. A free society is an economically productive society. The psalmist insists that Israel is to be a free society. In this way, the society is committed to the idea that God can raise up a poor person and place him in the company of kings. *Productivity is the distinguishing factor of a humanistic free society*. According to the psalmist, the sovereignty of God is the distinguishing feature of a biblical society.

---

1. Gary North, *Priorities and Dominion: An Economic Commentary on Matthew*, 2nd ed. (Dallas, Georgia: Point Five Press, [2000] 2012), ch. 47.

# 32

## A PRAYER FOR WIDESPREAD WEALTH

*That our garners may be full, affording all manner of store: that our sheep may bring forth thousands and ten thousands in our streets: That our oxen may be strong to labour; that there be no breaking in, nor going out; that there be no complaining in our streets. Happy is that people, that is in such a case: yea, happy is that people, whose God is the LORD.*

PSALM 144:13–15

This passage appears as part of a prayer to a sovereign God. The psalmist asks God to deliver him from evil people—specifically, strange children (v. 11). Then he asks that Israel's sons will be as plants grown up in their youth, and that daughters will be as cornerstones. This prayer has to do with inheritance. He seeks liberation from rule by strangers. He calls for an inheritance for the children of Israel.

Then comes a prayer regarding agricultural blessings. The psalmist asks that Israel's granaries be full (v. 12). The granaries should contain all manner of stores. This means that they should contain many kinds of grain. The psalmist wants a variety of grains in his diet. He also asks that their sheep would multiply. He wants not merely thousands of sheep but tens of thousands in the streets (v. 13). He wants visible overflowing. He also wants strong oxen to do work. He wants no breaking in or going out. In other words, he wants the oxen penned in and safe. He asks that there will be no complaining in the streets, meaning the community.

He closes the psalm with a declaration: "Happy is that people, that is in such a case: yea, happy is that people, whose God is the Lord" (v. 15). *He equates happiness with national wealth.* He is saying, in no uncertain terms, that having overflowing granaries, tens of thousands of sheep in the streets, and strong oxen are all aspects of a society in which there should be no complaining, due to happiness.

## A. The Pursuit of Happiness

Today, this psalm may appear to run counter to the New Testament's principle that men should not pursue great riches. This principle is also declared in the Proverbs. "Remove far from me vanity and lies: give me neither poverty nor riches; feed me with food convenient for me: Lest I be full, and deny thee, and say, Who is the Lord? or lest I be poor, and steal, and take the name of my God in vain" (Prov. 30:8–9).[1] Yet it sounds from this psalm as though great wealth per capita is an advantage worth praying for. It is an advantage that will produce happiness among the people. Why should increased wealth produce happiness? We are told that money cannot buy happiness, but it appears from these verses that grain, sheep, and oxen can buy happiness.

The psalmist is describing a free society. There are no foreign oppressors. There are no domestic oppressors. Sons and daughters inherit. Per capita wealth increases. *The marks of liberty involve economic growth.* Elsewhere in the psalms, we read that the pursuit of knowledge regarding the law of God is the basis of liberty. "And I will walk at liberty: for I seek thy precepts" (Psalm 119:45). This being the case, liberty under God should prove to be productive. *Covenant-keeping leads to greater per capita wealth.* This is the message of the early sections of Leviticus 26 and Deuteronomy 28. There is a cause-and-effect system in which conformity to biblical law produces increased per capita wealth. The psalmist understands this, and so he prays that God will bring to pass that which He had promised in Leviticus 26 and Deuteronomy 28. *The psalmist is calling on God to defend His covenant.* He is calling on God to do what He said he would do in Deuteronomy 8: bless His covenant people with great economic blessings so as to confirm the covenant (vv. 17–18).[2]

Any attempt to separate covenant-keeping from predictable prosperity runs against the words of this psalm. Any attempt to say that obedience to God's law produces poverty is an affront to what God has revealed regarding His covenant. Any attempt to say that the economic outcome of widespread covenant-keeping is random also flies in the face of Deuteronomy 26, Deuteronomy 28, and Psalm 144. Yet Bible commentators and especially theologians have argued that

---

1. Gary North, *Wisdom and Dominion: An Economic Commentary on Proverbs* (Dallas, Georgia: Point Five Press, [2007] 2012), ch. 85.

2. Gary North, *Inheritance and Dominion: An Economic Commentary on Deuteronomy,* 2nd ed. (Dallas, Georgia: Point Five Press, [1999] 2012), chaps. 21, 22.

there is no relationship between covenant-keeping and economic success in the New Covenant. They have argued that covenant-keeping produces either random results in terms of the specific blessings set forth in Leviticus 26 and Deuteronomy 28,[3] or else it produces the opposite results that are set forth in Leviticus 26 and Deuteronomy 28.[4]

The Christian church has labored for almost 2000 years under the instruction of theologians who have been hostile to economic growth as a mark of God's covenant blessings to those who obey His law. There has also been great hostility to biblical law. There has even been hostility to economic growth. There has been open hostility to the pursuit of profit. There has been hostility to merchants and businessmen. This hostility to ethical cause and effect in the realm of economic production restricted economic growth until the late eighteenth century. Christianity was not forthright in its advocacy of the kind of prayer that we find in Psalm 144. There has also been a disconnect between the covenantal framework of the Mosaic Covenant and what is presumed to be the covenantal framework of the New Covenant. It is widely assumed that there is been a total discontinuity between the two covenants. This means that Christians have rejected the testimony of Leviticus 26 and Deuteronomy 28. They have therefore also rejected the testimony of Psalm 144. Theologians for over a millennium praised poverty as a goal for the spiritual elite, which includes religious orders bound together by vows of poverty. Theologians within the Eastern Orthodox and Roman Catholic traditions have praised these religious orders as being superior to the common realm of business. This attitude has negatively affected economic theory within Christian circles.

## Conclusion

Psalm 144 is a declaration of independence from strange children (v. 11). It is also a declaration of independence from spiritual children, who do not recognize, accept, and proclaim the continuing authority of the Mosaic law regarding God's promised blessings for covenant-keeping.

---

3. This is Meredith G. Kline's position. See Chapter 27.
4. This is Cornelius Van Til's position. *Ibid.*

# 33

# THE FOUNDATION OF CONFIDENCE

*The* LORD *upholdeth all that fall, and raiseth up all those that be bowed down. The eyes of all wait upon thee; and thou givest them their meat in due season. Thou openest thine hand, and satisfiest the desire of every living thing.*

PSALM 145:14–16

## A. The Source of Strength

This passage affirms the comprehensive sovereignty of God over the affairs of this world: point one of the biblical covenant.[1] God imposes predictable sanctions: point four. [2]

The psalmist begins with an affirmation that God upholds all things that fall, and He also raises up all things that are bowed down. *This is an affirmation of faith in a God who protects covenant-keepers from disaster.* When covenant-keepers fall, God raises them up. Therefore, they should not lose faith in the efficacy of their efforts. The psalmist is speaking of covenant-keepers, not covenant-breakers. God does not raise up all those covenant-breakers who are bowed down. On the contrary, He structures the world so that covenant-breakers are subjected to negative sanctions.

Verse 15 is widely recited in formal church liturgies. "The eyes of all wait upon thee; and thou givest of them of their meat in due season." God provides sustenance for all the living creatures of the world. "Thou openest thine hand, and satisfiest the desire of every

---

1. Ray R. Sutton, *That You May Prosper: Dominion By Covenant*, 2nd ed. (Tyler, Texas: Institute for Christian Economics, [1987] 1992), ch. 1. Gary North, *Unconditional Surrender: God's Program for Victory*, 5th ed. (Powder Springs, Georgia: American Vision, [1980] 2010), ch. 1.
2. Sutton, ch. 4, North, ch. 4.

living thing" (v. 16). This does not mean that every living thing lives until a ripe old age. The desire of one creature may involve the loss of life of another creature. Verse 16 must therefore be interpreted in terms of the provision of life for every living thing, while it lives. Every species survives only when it finds sustenance in its environmental niche. Not all species survive. Millions of them have perished.[3] There is no guarantee of survival for every species under the authority of mankind. Only man is guaranteed survival by God.

The psalmist knew that members of a particular species survive through consuming members of a different species. This insight is not limited to modern man. What, then, is the psalmist attempting to convey? He is affirming the comprehensive authority of God over all living creatures. He is saying that no creature receives a benefit that God has not provided. God is the source of all life. God sustains all living creatures. No creature is autonomous. Every creature is dependent on God. "He giveth to the beast his food, and to the young ravens which cry" (Psalm 147:9). If every living creature is dependent on God, then this includes mankind. The psalmist is making a point: *men should acknowledge that God is the source of all their benefits.* God is the source of their protection. This is the God who upholds the covenant-keeper who falls. This is the God who protects those who were covenanted to Him.

The psalmist then says that "the Lord is nigh unto all them that call upon him, to all that call upon him in truth" (v. 18). This is not an indiscriminate promise to mankind in general. This is a promise to covenant-keepers who call upon God in truth. "He will fulfill the desire of them that fear him: he also will hear their cry, and will save them" (v. 19). Again, this is not an indiscriminate promise of benefits in history. These are covenantal promises. "The LORD preserveth all them that love him: but all the wicked will he destroy" (v. 20). *There are covenantal curses to match covenantal blessings.* This psalm affirms the system of ethical causation that is found in Leviticus 26 and Deuteronomy 28. The psalmist affirms God's sovereignty and therefore His ability to fulfill His promises. The promises that matter most, the psalmist implies, are the promises given to covenant-keepers. God also promises to undermine covenant-breakers. This system of sanctions favors those who confess faith in the God described by the psalmist.

---

3. Kenneth J. Hsu, *The Great Dying* (New York: Harcourt Brace Jovanovich, 1986).

## B. A Covenantal World

The psalmist moves from the general to the particular. He moves from God's upholding of all creatures to His upholding of covenant-keepers. God not only sustains the universe, He sustains covenant-keepers who seek to extend the kingdom of God in history. His *general sovereignty* is invoked by the psalmist in order to increase people's faith in His *specific sovereignty*. He favors covenant-keepers, and He disfavors covenant-breakers.

The psalmist affirms that the world is structured in terms of God's covenant. The creation is not ethically neutral. God structures it so that covenant-keepers prosper, while covenant-breakers do not. The world is not cosmically impersonal. It is entirely personal.[4] God sovereignly controls all of it.

This outlook is antithetical to modern economic theory. It asserts that the universe is not ethically impersonal. It affirms ethical principles, which are embodied in biblical law. The world is not neutral. It is not a level playing field. It is a tilted playing field. It is tilted in favor of covenant-keepers.

The psalmist is encouraging covenant-keepers to be confident in the face of adversity. Their God will lift them up if they should fall. Their God provides meat in due season for the entire creation. He is certainly capable of providing it for covenant-keepers. God opens His hand and satisfies the desire of every living thing. He will surely satisfy the desire of covenant-keepers who faithfully work to extend the kingdom of God in history. Those who oppose them will face negative sanctions from God.

This is an outlook that favors a vision of victory. God has not stacked the deck against covenant-keepers. On the contrary, God has stacked the deck against covenant-breakers. This is why the long run belongs to representatives of this God.

This mental outlook favors entrepreneurship. It favors the individual who is confident about his ability to satisfy consumer demand. He expects to make a profit. He expects to use this profit to fund further business ventures. He believes that even if he loses his fortune, God will nevertheless intervene again and uphold him in his attempt to make a new fortune. This is not a matter of luck; it is a matter of covenantal obedience.

---

4. Gary North, *Sovereignty and Dominion: An Economic Commentary on Genesis* (Dallas, Georgia: Point Five Press, [1982] 2012), ch. 1.

## God's controls All things
## Conclusion

This psalm affirms God's comprehensive oversight of history. He sustains all living things. There is nothing outside His control. This outlook is supposed to produce confidence. Covenant-keepers are to have confidence that their efforts will offset and overcome the efforts of covenant-breakers.

## A vision of Victory

He expects to make a profit.
He expects to use this profit
to fund other business ventures.
He believes that even if he loses
his fortune, God will intervene
Again & uphold him in his
Attempt to make A new fortune.
Not luck — matter of covenantal
obedience

# 34

## SANCTIONS AND STIPULATIONS

*Happy is he that hath the God of Jacob for his help, whose hope is in the* LORD *his God: Which made heaven, and earth, the sea, and all that therein is: which keepeth truth for ever: Which executeth judgment for the oppressed: which giveth food to the hungry. The* LORD *looseth the prisoners: The* LORD *openeth the eyes of the blind: the* LORD *raiseth them that are bowed down: the* LORD *loveth the righteous: The* LORD *preserveth the strangers; he relieveth the fatherless and widow: but the way of the wicked he turneth upside down.*

PSALM 146:5—9

The psalmist praises God as the creator who made heaven and earth. He is also the God who keeps truth forever. With this as background, the psalmist goes on to say that God executes judgment for the oppressed, gives food to the hungry, and releases the prisoners (v. 7). He says that the Lord preserves strangers and relieves orphans and widows (v. 9). God also turns the way of the wicked upside down (v. 9). The psalmist ends the psalm with an affirmation that God will reign forever (v. 10).

### A. Creator and Judge

The psalmist identifies God as the Creator and Judge. God is sovereign, and God imposes historical sanctions. God is a covenantal ruler. He intervenes in history to provide judgment for the oppressed and give food to the hungry.

The psalmist does not believe in a neutral universe. He believes in a universe which is totally under the sovereignty of God. This God operates in terms of ethical standards. He intervenes in history to execute judgment for the oppressed. Civil rulers who use civil law to oppress people can be sure that they will not escape the judgment of God.

144

The psalmist indicates that God intervenes to defend victims of oppression in the same way that He intervenes to help the hungry. In verse eight, he says that the Lord loves righteousness. God therefore intervenes to help the poor, the powerless, the orphan, and the widow. These categories are familiar to anyone who is familiar with the Mosaic law. Strangers, orphans, and widows, along with the poor, are models of the powerless in the Mosaic law. These people are easily victimized. Throughout the Mosaic law, God tells his people that He intervenes in history on behalf of victimized individuals.

The focus of this psalm is civil government. There can be unjust civil government. The Mosaic law promises that God will intervene to defend victims of unrighteous civil government. "Ye shall not afflict any widow, or fatherless child. If thou afflict them in any wise, and they cry at all unto me, I will surely hear their cry; And my wrath shall wax hot, and I will kill you with the sword; and your wives shall be widows, and your children fatherless" (Ex. 22:22–24).[1] The psalmist affirms this teaching in this psalm. It serves as a warning to magistrates who use the civil law to harm the innocent. It also offers hope to the innocent that God will intervene in history on their behalf.

This passage is favorable to judicial reform. But what kind of reform? The psalmist echoes the Mosaic law. The Mosaic law said that the civil government should not be used to oppress the innocent.[2] They may be weak, but they have a strong defender: God. Moses wrote down the laws that should govern civil government. It is the task of civil magistrates to enforce this law-order. When a society's legal order conforms to the standards of the Mosaic law, there is justice. The psalmist warns covenant-breakers that God intervenes on behalf of victims of the legal order which does not conform to biblical law.

## B. No Welfare State

This passage says nothing about taxation to raise funds to be distributed to the poor. It says nothing about tax policy. It does say that people can be oppressed. It says that there are hungry people, and God feeds them. It does not call on the civil government to feed them. To use passages that are favorable to the oppressed and the poor is legitimate when the critic of the prevailing social order has identified laws and practices that break the laws of the Mosaic covenant. But

---

1. Gary North, *Authority and Dominion: An Economic Commentary on Exodus* (Dallas, Georgia: Point Five Press, 2012), Part 3, *Tools of Dominion* (1990), ch. 48.
2. *Idem.*

*Mosaic law not language of social justice*

this is not what Social Gospel interpreters conclude about passages such as this one. They ignore the Mosaic law, and they emphasize the language of God's judgment. They see that God threatens negative sanctions against evildoers, but they do not go to the Mosaic law in order to find what God has said constitutes evildoing. *They invoke the language of social justice, but they do not cite the Mosaic law in order to discover what social justice is.* They use the language of outrage by the psalmists or by the prophets, but they do not invoke the standards that the psalmists and the prophets said were being violated. They call on civil magistrates to impose sanctions against evildoers, but they do not rely on the Mosaic law to identify the stipulations that the sanctions are supposed to enforce.

The Mosaic law does not lay down rules that would lead to a welfare state. There is no indication in the Mosaic law that the civil government is to be an agency for the redistribution of wealth from rich people to poor people, or from middle-class people to poor people. The only redistribution that the state calls for is restitution to victims of crime by the criminals who committed the crimes.[3] This is not the same as a welfare state. This is not taxation of the rich simply because they are rich, nor is it the transfer of state funds to the poor simply because they are poor. No such system of civil government appears in the Old Testament. Yet the psalmists and the profits invoked the language of God's judgment. It is deceptive to invoke the psalms or the prophetic books in a civil reform leading to a legal order that is opposed to Mosaic law.

*No welfare state*

## Conclusion

The psalmist identifies God as both Creator and Judge. God defends the victims of oppression. The psalmist warns that God brings negative sanctions against evildoers and positive sanctions for victims of oppression. He echoes the Mosaic law on this point. To appropriate the psalmist's praise of God for His support of the oppressed without also invoking the Mosaic law, which served to define oppression, is deceptive. It promotes civil oppression by promoting a legal order in opposition to the stipulations of the Mosaic law.

---

3. *Ibid.*, ch. 33. Cf. Gary North, *Victim's Rights: The Biblical View of Civil Justice* (Tyler, Texas: Institute for Christian Economics, 1990).

# 35

## SPECIALLY REVEALED STATUTES

*He sheweth his word unto Jacob, his statutes and his judgments unto Israel. He hath not dealt so with any nation: and as for his judgments, they have not known them. Praise ye the LORD.*

PSALM 147:19–20

The theocentric issue here is God as the law-giver. The psalmist affirms that God showed his word to Jacob and His statutes and his judgments to Israel. This is poetic language, since Jacob and Israel are two names for the same person. The psalmist makes this statement in the context of listing God's gifts to Israel. Psalm 147 is a song of praise. It lists things that God has done for His people. He makes peace on Israel's borders (v. 14). He provides snow (v. 16). He melts the ice (v. 18).

With this as background, the psalmist describes God's gift of His law. Not only has He showed his word to Jacob and His statutes to Israel, He has shown them to no one else. "He hath not dealt so with any nation: and as for his judgments, they have not known them. Praise ye the Lord" (v. 20). God has dealt in a special way with the nation of Israel, and *the mark of this special dealing with Israel is the Mosaic law*. This is how the psalmist ends psalm 147. The Israelites are to praise the Lord because of two things: He has shown His statutes to Israel, and He has not shown them to any other nation. Israel possesses a monopoly of justice.

When the prophets came before the nations of Israel and Judah, they called the people and the rulers back to the Mosaic law. The nation had violated this law, and the prophets came to the entire nation to warn them that judgment was coming. Centuries before, psalmists

147

had proclaimed the way of the Lord by proclaiming the way of the Mosaic law. The psalmists and the prophets warned the rulers of Israel not to oppress the people. The way to oppress the people, as the psalmists and the prophets said repeatedly, was to ignore the Mosaic law. Because the nation had ignored the Mosaic law, God promised to send the nation into captivity, the prophets warned.

To discuss the *message* of the psalmists and the prophets without relating this message to the *stipulations of the Mosaic covenant* is to practice deception. Such an analysis leads to the conclusion that the Mosaic law was not basic to the psalmists and the prophets. It implies that there can be social reform and political reform that is pleasing to God, but which has no relation to the Mosaic law. Such a proclamation is an attempt to mobilize covenant-keepers behind a political agenda whose details are not in conformity with the Mosaic law. It is an attempt to encourage Christians to work toward legal reform, but without going to the Bible in search of the legal categories and stipulations that constitute civic justice, according to the psalmists and the prophets. It is an attempt to invoke the authority of Psalms and the prophetic books in the name of God the Creator and God the Judge, but to abandon the specific laws by which He distinguished the nation of Israel from all the other nations.

The attempt by defenders of the Social Gospel to invoke the authority of Psalms and the prophetic books in the name of some version of socialist wealth redistribution reveals their hidden agenda. Their hidden agenda is to use the monopolistic power of the civil government to force their political opponents to pay for tax-funded programs that benefit their political constituents. It is an attempt to use the power of civil government to transfer wealth from one group to another group. This is done in the name of Christian charity, Christian justice, and Christian reform. Yet if the reforms do not conform to the stipulations of the Mosaic law, there is no biblical judicial basis for invoking the authority of Psalms and the prophetic books to support the political agenda of the Social Gospel.

I have surveyed those passages in Psalms that relate to economics. None of these passages has anything to do with the Social Gospel. On the contrary, the Social Gospel is antithetical to the system of private property which the Mosaic law established and which Psalms defends.[1]

---

1. Joel McDurmon, *God Versus Socialism: A Biblical Critique of the New Social Gospel* (Powder Springs, Georgia: American Vision, 2009).

## Conclusion

God's Bible-revealed laws are the tools of dominion.[2] The psalmist announces that God's gift of this law-order to Jacob constitute the basis for praise. This affirms that the laws of God offer a great benefit to the society that adopts them. They also provide a great benefit to any individual who follows them. *This benefit is dominion.* God blesses covenant-keepers.

Faith in this ethical system of cause and effect offers hope to covenant-keepers. They can extend God's kingdom in history by obeying God's Bible-revealed laws. God will reward obedience with blessings, including economic blessings. Covenant-keepers therefore possess a sure basis of confidence, just so long as they take the attitude of the author of Psalm 119.

> I will meditate in thy precepts, and have respect unto thy ways. I will delight myself in thy statutes: I will not forget thy word. Deal bountifully with thy servant, that I may live, and keep thy word (Psalm 119:15–17).

*Message of the Psalm and Prophets must be based on the stipulations of the Mosaic Covenant "Otherwise it is deception"*

*Implies there can be social justice social reform & political reform that is pleasing to God which has no relation to the Mosaic Law.*

---

2. Gary North, *Authority and Dominion: An Economic Commentary on Exodus* (Dallas, Georgia: Point Five Press, 2012), Part 3, *Tools of Dominion* (1990).

# CONCLUSION

*Ask of me, and I shall give thee the heathen for thine inheritance, and the utter-most parts of the earth for thy possession.*

PSALM 2:8

## A. Legitimate Confidence

Much of the Book of Psalms is devoted to the theme of confidence-building. The psalmists call on covenant-keepers to accept biblical law and obey it. If God's people do this, they will be upheld super-naturally by God.[1]

This form of confidence is not *self*-confidence. It rests on faith in the predictability of God's sanctions in history: the fourth point of the biblical covenant.[2] These sanctions are in turn governed by the laws of the covenant: the third point.[3] The Mosaic laws and the Mosaic sanctions were a unit under the Old Covenant. God promised in His law to intervene on behalf of the victims of evil practices, especially civil court practices, that ignored the Mosaic law.

> Thou shalt neither vex a stranger, nor oppress him: for ye were strangers in the land of Egypt. Ye shall not afflict any widow, or fatherless child. If thou afflict them in any wise, and they cry at all unto me, I will surely hear their cry; And my wrath shall wax hot, and I will kill you with the sword; and your wives shall be widows, and your children fatherless (Ex. 22:21–24).

The Book of Psalms reinforces this declaration.

---

1. Chapters 6, 33.

2. Ray R. Sutton, *That You May Prosper: Dominion By Covenant*, 2nd ed. (Tyler, Texas: Institute for Christian Economics, [1987] 1992), ch. 4. Gary North, *Unconditional Surrender: God's Program for Victory*, 5th ed. (Powder Springs, Georgia: American Vision, 2010), ch. 4.

3. *Ibid.*, ch. 3. North, ch. 4.

Covenant-keepers have a legitimate reason for their confidence regarding the positive outcome of their labors: the covenant itself. The psalmist says that individuals are blessed when they walk in God's counsel. This is not limited to corporate blessings. These are individual blessings. Obedience to biblical laws produces wealth.[4] Cause and effect are ethical.[5] *This system of ethical causation is the foundation of predictability in history.* It is the basis of Christian confidence regarding the future of God's kingdom in history.[6]

### B. Inheritance and Disinheritance

The psalms describe history as a dual process of inheritance and disinheritance: the fifth point of the biblical covenant.[7] This inheritance is comprehensive. It includes culture. The Messiah is the lawful heir in history. His representatives will inherit on His behalf.[8] God directs the inheritance. Covenant-keepers are told by the psalmist that this inheritance in history is as reliable as God's word. Poverty is not the inheritance of covenant-keepers. The wicked shall be cut off in history.[9] Their heaping up of riches is in vain. Their legacy will be dissipated.[10] He who trusts in riches has misplaced his confidence.[11]

The historical model for the disinheritance of the wicked is the defeat of the Canaanites by Israel. The lands of the heathen were inherited by Israel. This inheritance was comprehensive. Israel inherited everything.[12] Covenant-keepers will inherit the inheritance of the heathen in history. This is inheritance through disinheritance.[13]

This is why the psalmist prays for wealth.[14] This is an aspect of the inheritance.

### C. Success and Failure

Covenant-breakers have a rival view of the foundation of success in history: power. God's covenant establishes a different principle: *ethics over power.* God rules on the basis of His office as Creator. He rules

---

4. Chapter 28.
5. Chapter 1.
6. Chapter 20.
7. Sutton, *That You May Prosper*, ch. 5. North, *Unconditional Surrender*, ch. 5.
8. Chapter 2.
9. Chapter 6.
10. Chapter 7.
11. Chapter 9.
12. Chapter 22.
13. Chapter 22.
14. Chapter 32.

by means of His law.[15] He is the sovereign Owner. This is point one of the biblical covenant.[16] He is autonomous. He alone possesses this attribute. Autonomy is an incommunicable attribute. All ownership is therefore theocentric. Men do not own themselves; God does.[17] God delegates to stewards the responsibility of managing His property on earth and in time.[18] This is point two of the biblical covenant: representation.[19]

God is the source of water, which sustains life. This fact denies the autonomy of nature.[20] God brings water or removes it. This is an aspect of the great reversal.[21]

The psalmist insists that foreign kings will bring their offerings to the temple. This is also an aspect of the great reversal. The weak will triumph over the strong.[22] God protects the weak and defenseless.[23] God defends the poor defendant.[24] Corrupt judges should understand this. It should frighten them.[25]

This warning indicates that covenant-breakers can triumph for a time. The wicked prosper. The psalmist admits that this bothered him. But he came to his senses. God is merely placing them in slippery places. Their downfall is assured.[26]

The comprehensive triumph in history by covenant-keepers will be visible. This victory will grieve the wicked. They will melt away. They will lose influence.[27]

The entrepreneur must conquer his fear of failure. Psalm 107 describes men who face waves on the sea. Covenant-keepers learn that God delivers them.[28]

### D. Optimism and Pessimism

Confidence is basic to entrepreneurship. Entrepreneurship involves predicting the economic future and then acting in the present to meet

---

15. Chapter 3.
16. Sutton, *That You May Prosper*, ch. 1.
17. Chapter 10.
18. Chapter 5.
19. Sutton, *That You May Prosper*, ch. 2.
20. Chapter 12.
21. Chapter 25.
22. Chapter 14.
23. Chapters 18, 34.
24. Chapter 26.
25. Chapter 21.
26. Chapter 17.
27. Chapter 30.
28. Chapter 24.

future consumer demand at a competitive price. The goal is to buy low and sell high. This mental and emotional outlook requires confidence: in the future, in cause and effect, in one's abilities. Psalms insists that this confidence is mandatory for covenant-keepers.[29]

Pessimism about the future stifles entrepreneurship. When this pessimism is applied to culture in general, it leads to withdrawal and paralysis. Normal people do not commit to projects to transform a culture if they believe that they and those who share their views cannot win.

The psalms bring a message of confidence. They are filled with hope. They prophesy comprehensive victory for covenant-keepers.

The Book of Psalms is more openly optimistic than any other book in the Bible. It affirms that covenant-keepers will inherit civilization as surely as Israel inherited Canaan, which is the model of biblical inheritance in terms of its comprehensive character. There is therefore no book in the Bible more opposed to amillennialism. While premillennialists can consistently appropriate the Psalms' message of comprehensive inheritance, applying it to a discontinuous future millennial era, amillennialists must interpret the psalms of inheritance and victory as applying to the world beyond the final judgment. Until that day, covenant-breakers inherit, because they are in charge today and will be in charge tomorrow. How can such a view of eschatology be reconciled with the Psalms?

> He hath given meat unto them that fear him: he will ever be mindful of his covenant. He hath shewed his people the power of his works, that he may give them the heritage of the heathen (Psalm 111:5–6).

> Let the saints be joyful in glory: let them sing aloud upon their beds. Let the high praises of God be in their mouth, and a two-edged sword in their hand; To execute vengeance upon the heathen, and punishments upon the people; To bind their kings with chains, and their nobles with fetters of iron; To execute upon them the judgment written: this honour have all his saints. Praise ye the LORD (Psalm 149:5–9)

---

29. Chapter 27.

### E. Inequality Forever

There is no equality in hell.[30] There is no equality in heaven. There is no equality in history.[31]

This system of ethical cause and effect is affirmed in the Mosaic law. It appears in a concise form in Leviticus 26 and Deuteronomy 28. The psalmists invoked this system of causation. So did the prophets.[32]

The Book of Psalms does not advocate a system of economic equality. It predicts a series of reversals. Dry land will become watered; productive land will become barren.[33] A great reversal is coming: the powerful will bring tribute to the weak.[34] Evildoers will be trapped by their own devices.[35] This, too, was set forth in the Mosaic law as the ideal.

> The LORD shall open unto thee his good treasure, the heaven to give the rain unto thy land in his season, and to bless all the work of thine hand: and thou shalt lend unto many nations, and thou shalt not borrow. And the LORD shall make thee the head, and not the tail; and thou shalt be above only, and thou shalt not be beneath; if that thou hearken unto the commandments of the LORD thy God, which I command thee this day, to observe and to do them: And thou shalt not go aside from any of the words which I command thee this day, to the right hand, or to the left, to go after other gods to serve them (Deut. 28:12–14).

There is nothing in the Book of Psalms that supports the statist theology known as the Social Gospel, let alone Marxist-tinged Liberation Theology. There is not one word about the state as an agency of

---

30. "And that servant, which knew his lord's will, and prepared not himself, neither did according to his will, shall be beaten with many stripes. But he that knew not, and did commit things worthy of stripes, shall be beaten with few stripes. For unto whomsoever much is given, of him shall be much required: and to whom men have committed much, of him they will ask the more" (Luke 12:47–48). Gary North, *Treasure and Dominion: An Economic Commentary on Luke*, 2nd ed. (Dallas, Georgia: Point Five Press, [2000] 2012), ch. 28.

31. "Now if any man build upon this foundation gold, silver, precious stones, wood, hay, stubble; Every man's work shall be made manifest: for the day shall declare it, because it shall be revealed by fire; and the fire shall try every man's work of what sort it is. If any man's work abide which he hath built thereupon, he shall receive a reward. If any man's work shall be burned, he shall suffer loss: but he himself shall be saved; yet so as by fire" (I Cor. 3:12–15). Gary North, *Judgment and Dominion: An Economic Commentary on First Corinthians*, 2nd. ed.(Dallas, Georgia: Point Five Press, [2001] 2012), ch. 3.

32. Gary North, *Restoration and Dominion: An Economic Commentary on the Prophets* (Dallas, Georgia: Point Five Press, 2012).

33. Chapter 25.

34. Chapter 14.

35. Chapter 4.

wealth redistribution. There are invocations for justice, but justice is always defined in terms of the Mosaic law.

> Ye shall do no unrighteousness in judgment: thou shalt not respect the person of the poor, nor honour the person of the mighty: but in righteousness shalt thou judge thy neighbour (Lev. 19:15).

## Conclusion

The Book of Psalms proclaims victory in history for covenant-keepers. It announces the process of inheritance in history. Inheritance is ethical. This is affirmed in the Book of Deuteronomy, but it is affirmed far more eloquently and far more decisively in the Book of Psalms.

This should give covenant-keepers confidence. Their efforts in history will bear fruit in history. The efforts of covenant-breakers will be overwhelmed in history. There is not one word in the Book of Psalms about the final judgment and the world that will follow. *The psalms are entirely earth-bound and history-bound*. They do not talk about pie in the sky by and by. They talk about life on earth in history. They talk about pie on earth for covenant-keepers, and dregs for covenant-breakers. They talk about continuity for those who are meek before God, who will inherit the earth.

# NOTES

# NOTES

# NOTES

# NOTES

# NOTES

Made in the USA
Middletown, DE
22 July 2023